Hermann Finch 1975

The
Hermann
Rusch
Greenbrier
Cookbook

The Hermann Rusch Greenbrier Cookbook

Hermann G. Rusch with Martina Neely

HENRY REGNERY COMPANY • CHICAGO

Library of Congress Cataloging in Publication Data

Rusch, Hermann G.
    The Hermann Rusch Greenbrier Cookbook

    Includes index.
    1. Cookery.   I. Neely, Martina, joint author.
II. Title.
TX715.R957   641.5   74-27825
ISBN 0-8092-8353-0

Published by Henry Regnery Company
180 North Michigan Avenue, Chicago, Illinois 60601
Manufactured in the United States of America
Library of Congress Catalog Card Number: 74-27825
International Standard Book Number: 0-8092-8353-0

Published simultaneously in Canada by
Fitzhenry & Whiteside Limited
150 Lesmill Road
Don Mills, Ontario M3B 2T5
Canada

CONTENTS

THE GREENBRIER TRADITION

Before the Civil War, Southern aristocracy was traditionally engaged in a whirlwind of cotillions, balls, and other elegant social activities. The scent of magnolia mingled with expensive imported perfumes. That romantic image of the Old South was erased by the winds of time and the clouds of war. Little from the past returned to most places after the conflict, and Southern society was, indeed, as Margaret Mitchell agonized, "a civilization gone with the wind."

But for a while, throughout the rugged Appalachian Mountains of the Virginias, there remained a few citadels of Southern tradition and romance that time and a more complicated society seemed to elude. The Greenbrier Hotel, nestled in a sylvan setting near White Sulphur Springs, West Virginia, is one of the few spots left where this romantic and elegant past has been preserved. The scent of flowering trees and bushes is still there, and if you squint just a little and let your imagination soar to the frescoed and chandeliered ballroom, you can see the flame of a thousand candles dance gaily, as a puff of crisp evening air sweeps quietly through the open French doors. And you can see the costumed cavaliers and their belles promenading smartly through the lobbies.

1

All this was part of the tradition at The Greenbrier—as was champagne and watermelon on the lawn each spring. It was a society that had imported the spa atmosphere from Europe. Actually, The Greenbrier tradition began two years after the Declaration of Independence was signed, when the first recorded visitor came to what is now White Sulphur Springs, West Virginia, to "take the waters" of the spring. A charming legend says that it all began long before that, when an Indian brave and his maiden so loved the valley and its uncommon beauty that they chose to leave their tribe and stay there. They were blissful, finding their food in the sparkling streams and quiet forests that lay all around their peaceful valley; they were so happy that the Great Spirit became jealous and decided that they should be punished.

On a sunny summer's day, the maiden was picking wild flowers to weave into a garland for her sleeping lover when two arrows came zinging out of the sky. One pierced the heart of the sleeping brave, but the maiden, leaping to his side to save him, escaped the arrow that was meant for her heart. When she saw that her lover was dead, she screamed in anguish and ran to get the fallen arrow to plunge into her own heart. As she pulled it from the ground, out gushed the white sulphur springs. Heartbroken, she plunged the arrow into her heart and, once more, upset the plan of the Great Spirit.

The brave was buried with his feet toward the setting sun. His grave is now a small mountain called "The Sleeping Giant." The spirit of the maiden was doomed to walk the grounds of the springs until the spring runs dry. Unfortunately for the maiden, the spring shows no signs of going dry. It bubbles up through the rocks as bountifully as ever.

Today, guests enjoy the same vistas and mountain scenery that have been viewed by many of history's notables. For in the ensuing two centuries after the first visitor, White Sulphur Springs was host to Daniel Webster, Henry Clay, and Robert E. Lee. Along with them came nineteen presidents, including Dwight D. Eisenhower, John F. Kennedy, Richard Nixon, and Gerald R. Ford. There were other distinguished guests: King

Edward VIII, Princess Grace and Prince Rainier of Monaco, and Prime Minister Nehru of India.

It is difficult to walk the spacious manicured grounds of the 6,500-acre resort or to stroll through the lobbies without being caught up on wings of nostalgia. You can imagine the history that has preceded you. You can almost hear the singing coming from behind the colonnades of the President's Cottage as the Van Burens celebrated their son's wedding. You can see Henry Clay offering his arm to a belle as they began a march around a lobby. Others followed them, and a tradition was born: the "Treadmill," a promenade dance that was to continue for another century. You can picture President Tyler escorting his young bride, Julia, through the door of their cottage.

The affluent and the aristocratic came for the unmatched beauty of the country and for the Georgian elegance of the hotel. And they came for the healing powers of the water.

One such visitor, a small and nimble man, led a group in formal clothes down the seven steps to the springhouse—the trademark of the resort—filled his glass, and said, "I first tasted the water when I visited White Sulphur in 1919 as Prince of Wales." He paused, took a drink from the glass, made a face, and said, "It tastes just as bad now as it did then!" There was a ripple of laughter, a few joined in tasting the water, and the group began its merry trek back to the hotel, the Duke of Windsor in the lead.

There are a number of reasons for The Greenbrier mystique: the simple Indian legend, the believed curative powers of the springs, and its remoteness—a hideaway from a warring world, and a retreat from depressions, both imagined and real. But the real beginning was over a billion years ago when viscous currents deep within the earth's molten core began an erosion process that would one day send forth the bubbling mineral waters.

It was hope of a cure that first brought people to the springs. If you had walked some distance below the springs in 1778, you would have seen a woman, crippled with rheumatism, lying in a hollowed-out log. The family of Amanda Anderson, hearing that Indians believed these waters had miraculous curative powers, carried her there in a litter slung between two horses, for she was too ill to walk. Each day her kin filled the tree trough with spring water and heated it with hot stones. The treatment worked and her condition improved. The swollen joints grew limber again, and, when she left a few weeks later, she was astride her horse.

The Greeks were the first to recognize the value of mineral springs, but the Romans were the first to utilize them. The mineral spring at Spa, Belgium, was the source of the generic title that is given to such establishments. But it was The Greenbrier and other spas of the South that added the charm and gentility.

An inauspicious name, White Sulphur Springs, became associated with elegance the world over. Among the first settlers to explore the White Sulphur Springs vicinity were the French: the name *Ronceverte* appeared on Canadian maps some time before its equivalent, *Greenbrier,* was used on English maps. The town of Ronceverte is but a few miles away. Regardless of the language, the word referred to a brier that grows in tangled profusion in West Virginia. Greenbrier, bold brier, devil's clothesline, whichever of its names you use, White Sulphur naturalist Lyle Bryce once asserted, "it's a most troublesome bramble."

But *troublesome* wasn't the word Henry Clay associated with White Sulphur Springs on a warm July day in 1817 when he arrived with a servant and three horses for a visit that lasted three days. The ledger entry of this visit is worth recounting in detail for the picture it gives of those times. Clay's room and board cost $1.50 a night; lodging his servant and the three horses cost 75 cents each per night. Clay took away nine gallons of feed for his return trip, bought a dozen cigars (25 cents), and had his clothes laundered (68½ cents). His servant had three drinks: a dram of brandy upon arrival and two grogs (25 cents total). The grand total for three days was $16.51½. Henry Clay drank "hailstorms," an earlier version of the mint julep, as the guest of the hotel's proprietor.

White Sulphur Springs was gaining a reputation by the time of Clay's first visit. There were many reasons for its prosperity: the James River and the dusty Kanawha Turnpike wove past the springs; and people said that a wondrous thing happened there.

Some who had been drinking the white sulphur water found that silver coins in their pockets had turned black. Again the legend takes over. A southern Bobby Shaftoe was supposed to have walked near the springs and the silver buckles on his shoes tarnished. You see, unlike most other Virginia springs, the water had a noticeable sulphur odor.

The third reason for the success came from the customers' prosperity. During the 1820s, the prices paid for the South's cotton crops rose to new highs; so the wealthy plantation owners sought out halcyon settings in which to relax.

Tidewater epidemics of cholera and yellow fever in New Orleans caused people to look around for places that were unaffected, places where they could comfortably escape the dangers of the diseases. The Virginia springs were free from pestilence. Reasons be damned! Off to the springs! Those who visited these watering places for the first time found that the scenery and the sociability were to their liking.

Finally, the Southerner is a gregarious person, and the life, at least on plantations, gave few opportunities to mix with others of one's class. Visits to the springs even gave parents a chance to arrange suitable marriages for their daughters.

White Sulphur Springs afforded the aristocrats an opportunity to pass the summers like grand old Southern gentlemen of an earlier era. They came from Virginia and the tobacco plantations, from the rice and cotton plantations of South Carolina and Georgia, and from the sugar plantations of Louisiana. "There was the coachman and the ladies' maid, and sometimes a family cook, and a merry, dignified, proper time they had of it then," one chronicle reported. There was no schottische, no German, no round dancing, only the graceful Virginia reel. There was no strychnine, no adulterations, just a genuine home-distilled apple brandy, or pure port and Madeira of one's own importation. So they came to Greenbrier and spent money freely, and bought the fine Greenbrier horses to put to their carriages; and on the first day of September they went back to their places, to come again the next year.

A member of President Martin Van Buren's party described a

picnic on the lawn: "We found everything amply provided for us, as if it were by invisible hands. Invisible hands had got ready the most tempting and cooling beverages for the dusty, thirsty guests (it was a very dusty day), and invisible hands had prepared, under a large green arbor at the foot of the mountain, a most magnificent entertainment. And then with myrtle leaves for a canopy over our devoted heads, we all sat down with smiling faces to do justice to the delicacies spread before us. We had all the luxuries of the mountains, the farm-yard and the streams."

The spell was only slightly broken when the invisible hands turned out to belong to servants who had to "duel with the corks to the champagne." The table, however, "was sparkling with wine and wit."

A new grand hotel, built in 1858, was advertised as the largest building in the South and the largest hotel in the United States. The parlor was half again as big as the East Room of the White House. One overly enthusiastic journalist reported that the "dining room was so immense that waiters were forced to serve on horseback." This colossal building was dubbed the Grand Central Hotel. The spring's proprietors were fascinated by the words that expressed the hopes of hotel owners everywhere: *Grand Central*. But no one paid any attention. It became "The White" to guests, so called because of the spring. It *officially* became the "Old White" when the Chesapeake and Ohio Railway purchased the property in 1910.

There were hard times between Grand Central and Old White. A war was brewing, and when the White Sulphur Springs season began on June 1, 1860, the proprietors had installed a pistol gallery for the convenience of registered guests. The preoccupations of the elders affected the youth. Children, often led by young Charley Bonaparte, great-grand-nephew of Napoleon, marched on the lawn. He lived in Baltimore "E" cottage with his grandfather, Jerome Napoleon Bonaparte, who was suing in the French courts for an inheritance and recognition in the Bonaparte line of succession.

Even with the outbreak of the Civil War there was an 1861 season, although rates were reduced, "owing to the embarrassed state of the country." The season was cut short as troops of the Union and the Confederacy began to march through the area. General Robert E. Lee was one of the first military visitors. In fact, it was here that he first saw Traveller, the four-year-old-gray that was to become his favorite mount.

The war came close to erasing the Old White from the spa circuit. Union general David Hunter, whose forces included a Colonel Rutherford B. Hayes and a Captain William McKinley, took over the hotel at one point. After appraising the building, Hunter issued an order to burn everything upon his departure. A 25-year-old captain, Henry Algernon du Pont, knew of the rich heritage of the resort and influenced the general not to destroy the buildings. "If we have later to occupy and hold this country, the White Sulphur Springs will be the natural point for our principal station, as so many roads converge here. The buildings as they stand would furnish excellent winter quarters for at least a brigade of troops," he said to the general.

After the Civil War, the slow, painful rebuilding of Southern life began. Although heavily damaged, the Old White opened its doors, after two years of rebuilding, for the 1867 season. The *Richmond Dispatch* reported that "we cannot expect to see there the society that once gave life and gayety and grace to that incomparably delightful summer resort."

The paper was wrong. A man who was to help bring it back to its former position rode up the circuitous path in the summer of 1867. His white hair, beard, and wide-brimmed hat were trademarks that were familiar to his followers. His erect bearing and gray horse were well known throughout the nation. Robert E. Lee's influence was felt by everyone, Southerner and Northerner alike. His summers at the White Sulphur resort helped to dispel the gloom of a "lost cause" that surrounded even the spring.

One evening, Lee noticed two visitors, the wartime governor of Pennsylvania Andrew G. Curtin and his wife, sitting apart from the other guests. After inquiring why no one had invited the couple to join in the lively conversation of the other guests, Lee was informed, "Why, General, we assumed you would want to be alone with your *followers. We* certainly prefer that."

With that, the general rose and said, "In the presence of God, I must say that I have never known one moment of bitterness and resentment." And he strode across the floor to bring the Curtins to the other assembled guests. From that time on Southerners and Northerners at White Sulphur Springs talked to one another.

The Old White had seen sweetness, beauty and romance, cavaliers and beautiful women, but it was the years after the war that brought the era of the belles.

There was Mary Triplett, the woman for whom the last duel ever staged in the Virginias was fought. There was Irene Langhorne. Irene's belledom did not begin with a planned debut. She was sitting with others in one of the deep window bays of the ballroom when William Wright of Philadelphia came to stand in front of her. "How old are you, my dear?" he asked. "Sixteen," she replied. "Then it's time you were out." He lifted her down and they danced. Later she met and married Charles Dana Gibson and became the archetype of his famous Gibson Girl.

Affluence was obvious as guests began arriving in private railway cars. One car on the siding at the White Sulphur Springs station might belong to William K. Vanderbilt, another to J. Ogden Armour. Others might carry Astors, Dukes, Drexels, or Biddles.

Often the topic of what one's parents *did*—rather than the time-hallowed Southern topic of who one's parents *were*—was brought up. On one occasion, the young Mrs. Anna Washington Tucker was introduced to a group of women. After a few pleasantries, one asked Mrs. Tucker, "What does your father do?"

"Why, he's a farmer," she replied.

There was little conversation until she left the group, whereupon they set after her with a vengeance, because their fathers were all industrial tycoons.

"A farmer's girl at the Old White?" one said.

"What's this place coming to?" commented a Pittsburgh woman.

But this was too much for the woman who had performed the introductions. "I don't believe she told you the name of her farm," she said.

"No," yawned the Pittsburgh girl.

"Mount Vernon," the woman replied.

The champagne suppers and fancy dress balls became even more elaborate, and a new main hotel, officially named The Greenbrier, was built in 1913 by its new owners, the Chesapeake and Ohio Railway. It operated independently until 1922, when the Old White failed to pass a fire inspection and was ordered razed.

In the 25 years after The Greenbrier Hotel was built, things happened fast. The first 18-hole golf course was built in 1914. Today there are three 18-hole courses and 17 tennis courts. In 1929 an airport was built nearby, making the resort more accessible. Appropriately, one of the first persons to fly in was Amelia Earhart. In 1936 Sam Snead was named golf pro, a position he still holds.

During World War II, The Greenbrier, at the request of frequent guest Cordell Hull, Secretary of State, housed interned diplomats and foreign newspaper correspondents. The relative isolation of The Greenbrier made it easy to guard. On December 21, 1941, the first contingent of 159 Germans and Hungarians arrived. Further arrivals of German and Japanese swelled the total to 300.

By July 15, 1942, a prisoner exchange—the German and Japanese for American diplomats and newsmen being held at Bad Nauheim, a German mineral spa—took place, and the hotel once again opened for business.

But it had been open only one month when the army bought the property to be used as Ashford General Hospital. As many paintings and old engravings as possible were hastily carted off into storage, loaned to museums, or donated to Washington and Lee University. Other furnishings were auctioned. On August 29 a farewell mint julep party was held and tears flowed openly as guests of many seasons said their last good-byes to the famous old hotel.

Packed with history, The Greenbrier ended its first phase, which had begun in 1778. Fortunately a return to elegance began in 1948. The Chesapeake and Ohio Railway repurchased The

Greenbrier and brought in famed decorator Dorothy Draper. Enter the Greenbrier of today.

Mrs. Draper made her first inspection by flashlight because there was no electric power. It may have been because of the lack of electricity or because of the original design, but she felt the place was a Brobdingnagian monster of a bowling alley. There was a 20-foot-high passageway from the terrace dining room at one end of the building straight through to the President's parlor at the other end—a distance slightly over one-fifth mile. Mrs. Draper planned walls that would minimize the immense length of the building without cutting the public spaces into areas where guests would feel cramped. She ordered fireplaces and arches placed strategically to provide ever changing views as one walked from one lobby to another.

Historic furnishings of the old hotel, such as the Sheffield chandelier, the Queen Anne-style table in the President's parlor, antique mirrors, and splendid Czechoslovakian chandeliers, were rescued from storage and again put to use.

In the sleeping-floor corridors Mrs. Draper designed a rhododendron-patterned wallpaper, a salute to West Virginia's state flower. In the individual rooms, she created such a range of fabric, paint, and wallpaper choices that no two of the 650 rooms look exactly alike.

Life magazine described the grand opening party as the "most lavish party of the century." Fourteen private railroad cars and numerous private limousines and private airplanes carried luminaries such as the Duke and Duchess of Windsor, Prince and Princess Alexander Hohenlohe, the Marchioness of Hartington, Lady Stanley, Lady Cochran, Lady Harry Oakes, and Lady Sheila Milbank; the *Social Register's* Winthrop Aldrich, Mr. and Mrs. Anthony Biddle Duke, Mrs. Nicholas du Pont, Mrs. Harrison Williams, Mr. and Mrs. Winston Guest, and many others. The list of political VIPs was just as imposing.

Others included Pearl Mesta, Elsa Maxwell, William Randolph Hearst, Jr., J. Arthur Rank, and Bing Crosby, who claimed that the maid who cleaned his room used a mink mop and checked for dust with a lorgnette.

Raved Cholly Knickerbocker: "We doubt that even the Sultan of Turkey, the Emperor of China, or the Czar of Russia, when these fabulous courts were at their peak, ever attempted anything on a more colossal scale." Cleveland Amory, who seldom resorted to rave reviews, called it "the outstanding resort society function in modern social history."

For an encore, The Greenbrier transformed this opening party into an Annual Spring Festival.

To expand the services, a clinic was opened. It is a diagnostic clinic in a resort setting, designed for executives who are repelled by the atmosphere of a hospital. The clinic opened its doors specifically to provide examinations for the healthy.

Since The Greenbrier's reopening, there has been a steady increase in the number of facilities. The mineral baths were expanded, a gun club was built, and an outdoor swimming pool joined the indoor one. Automated bowling lanes and a motion picture theater were added. All three of The Greenbrier's 18-hole golf courses start and finish at the Golf and Tennis Club.

For those with scenery in mind, The Greenbrier stables provide a pair of high-stepping bays to pull an old-fashioned buckboard. Saddle horses are available for guests who want to follow the hoofprints of General Lee's Traveller along 200 miles of trails on the nearby mountains. Almost 40 miles of walking trails are also maintained.

At capacity, The Greenbrier can play host to 1,100 guests. But even with so great a load, their small city of 1,100 employees is unobtrusive. The Greenbrier continues to offer its heritage of fine service. Many of the employees carry on a family tradition of proud service that has lasted through many generations.

The late New York columnist Ward Morehouse put it this way: "I consider myself a connoisseur of hotels, having been a hotel guest in all 50 states, in all of the countries of South America, and in cities scattered across the world . . . And now I've come upon a hotel whose splendor outshines them all, The Greenbrier—the luxurious establishment at White Sulphur Springs. The Greenbrier is spotless and flawless, quite the most immaculate hotel in my experience . . . Bellmen are polite and expert; so are the doormen and telephone girls. Everybody speaks so softly The Greenbrier seems to be a house of whispers. It's nothing like the tumult of New York."

As part of a gastronomic tradition, The Greenbrier's staff of fifty chefs is directed by a European traditionalist, Swiss-born Hermann G. Rusch.

The Greenbrier's menus are designed to appeal to everyone. Even when a thousand dinners must be served, there are items on the menu that will not appeal to more than a handful of guests. *"Tripes a la Mode de Caen* may appeal to only six guests," says Rusch, "but the six hundred people who order shrimp cocktail and the filet mignon must be equally satisfied."

Hermann G. Rusch

The distinguished career of The Greenbrier's Executive Food Director, Hermann G. Rusch, began in 1924 at the Hotel d'Espagne in St. Croix when he was seventeen years of age. During the next ten years, he displayed his talents at outstanding hotels throughout Switzerland, Egypt, Sweden, and France.

A native of Appenzell, Switzerland, Mr. Rusch was born on September 26, 1907. He married Violet Loertscher in 1941, and they have four children, Gregory, Preston, Ronald (deceased), and Christopher.

Mr. Rusch is fluent in English, French, Italian, and German. He came to the United States in 1939 when he was appointed Chef Steward for the Swiss Pavilion at the New York World's Fair. He stayed to become Chef Steward at the Delmonico Hotel in New York. From there, he went to the Villa Margherita in Charleston, South Carolina, the Whitman Hotel in Miami Beach, the Belmont Plaza and the Lexington Hotel, both in New York. He came to The Greenbrier in 1955 as Executive Chef Steward. Two years later he was named Executive Food Director, a position he still holds.

Among the achievements and awards given to Hermann Rusch are:

Supervising Chef of the U.S.A. Olympic Committee

   1956   Olympic Games, Melbourne, Australia
   1959   Pan American Games, Chicago, Illinois
   1960   Winter Olympic Games, Squaw Valley, California
   1960   Olympic Games, Rome, Italy
   1963   Pan American Games, Sao Paulo, Brazil
   1964   Winter Olympic Games, Innsbruck, Austria
   1964   Olympic Games, Tokyo, Japan

Chairman of Food and Housing for the U.S. Olympic team

   1967   Pan American Games, Winnipeg, Canada
   1968   Winter Olympic Games, Grenoble, France
   1968   Olympic Games, Mexico City, Mexico

Director of Food Services

   1971   Pan American Games, Cali, Colombia
   1972   Winter Olympic Games, Sapporo, Japan
   1972   Olympic Games, Munich, Germany

Co-Chairman of Food and Housing

   1975   Pan American Games, Sao Paulo, Brazil
   1976   Winter Olympic Games, Innsbruck, Austria
   1976   Olympic Games, Montreal, Canada

Achievements

Gold Medal Z.I.K.A., International Exhibition, Zurich, 1930

Gold Medal Expositione de Alberghieri, Rome, Italy, 1932

Five-time Winner of Grand Prix at National Hotel Exposition
   New York

Two-time Winner of Prize of Honor, National Hotel Exposition
   New York

Winner of the Gold Medal of the Société Culinaire
    Philanthropique

Winner of the Gold Medal of the Academy Culinaire de Paris,
    France

Winner of the Silver Medal of the French Republic
    (highest award to the Culinary Profession)

Winner of the Gold Medal of the U.S. Culinary Federation

Citation Culinary Institute, New Haven, Connecticut
    (Graduation, 1954)

Winner of the DeBand Award, 1956 (for promotion
    of culinary arts)

Winner of the Partridge Oscar Award, 1957 (for promotion
    of elegant services)

Nominated Chef of the Golden Dozen, 1958

Recipient of the first Otto Gentsch Gold Medal, 1959

Appointed to the Honorable Order of the Kentucky Colonels
    by Governor Albert B. Chandler of Kentucky, 1958

Recipient of the first Caesar Ritz Award by the Society of
    Bacchus, 1966 (for maintaining the standards set by the
    man for whom this award has been named)

Winner of the Grand Prix for The Greenbrier, at the Concours
    de Tables Fleuries et Dressées, Cannes, France,
    Competition of 14 countries

Recipient of the Auguste Escoffier's "Gold Plaque" for
    educating young Americans in the culinary arts

Recipient of the "Eugene Lacroix" Medaille of Frankfurt,
    Germany, for inspiring the culinary arts profession in
    young culinarians

Professional Memberships

Past President of the Société Culinaire Philanthropique,
    New York, 1951-1956

Past National Treasurer, American Culinary Federation

Officer of the Les Amis D'Escoffier

Board of Governors of the American Culinary Federation

Corresponding member of the Culinary Academy of France

Chairman of the Chef de Cuisine Association of America,
     five years

Honorary member of the Epicurean Club, London, England

Honorary member of the Circle de Chef de Cuisine, Bern,
     Switzerland

Honorary member of the International Chef's Association,
     Frankfurt, Germany

Member of the Guild of Sommeliers and Society of Bacchus

Member of the Confrerie de la Chaine Des Rotisseurs

Member of the Confrerie de Gastronomie Normande

Honorary member of the Vatel Club, New York

Honorary member of the British Culinary Association

Honorary member of the Oesterreichischer Kochverband

Member of the French Culinary Academy

Member of the American National Council on Hotel and
     Restaurant Education

Member of La Triperie d'Or, France

Member of the Helvetia Association, U.S.A. and Switzerland

Member of the International Chef's Association of America

Chairman and Organizer of the American Team to the Culinary
     Olympic, in Bern, Switzerland — 18 participating nations.

Member of the Board, Culinary Institute of America, New
     Haven, Connecticut

Honorary member of the Chef's Association of Pittsburgh

Member of the International Steward's and Caterers'
     Association, Inc.

Honorary member of the Circle de Chef de Cuisine,
     Zurich, Switzerland

Other Honors

Chairman of the Jury, Culinary Exhibit, Norfolk, Virginia, 1958

Chairman of the Jury, Culinary Exhibit, Washington, D.C., in 1962, 1964, 1966, and 1968

Honorary chairman of Culinary Exhibit, New York City, since 1965

Chairman of judges, Culinary Arts Exposition, San Juan, Puerto Rico, 1967

Address to Cornell University Hotel School in 1967, Subject: "Olympic Catering"

Chairman of judges, Culinary Exhibit, Agricultural Exhibition, Hamilton, Bermuda, April, 1969 and 1971

Commencement Address, Graduation Exercises, The Culinary Institute of America, June 3, 1969

Address to The Academy of Chefs of America, Seattle, Washington, September, 1969
Subject: "Culinary Training and Professional Status"

Chairman of the judges, Seventh Culinary Arts Exposition, San Juan, Puerto Rico, October, 1969

Address for Hotel, Restaurant, and Institutional Management Seminar, Hospitality Weekend 1970, Michigan State University, April, 1970

Chairman of the judges committee, Culinary Show, National Restaurant Convention, Chicago, Illinois, May, 1971

Winner of the Silver Plate Award from the International Foodservice Association at the National Restaurant Exposition in Chicago, Illinois for "the best Foodservice Operation in 1971 in the Hotel Industry."

Nominated Honorary Citizen of West Virginia by Governor Arch A. Moore, 1971

La Médaille du Mérit Agricole from the French Government. The highest award to the Culinary Profession for forwarding education in the culinary arts, 1972

Chairman of the panel of judges for the International
    Food Festival, Atlanta, Georgia, where the Hermann G.
    Rusch Culinary Arts Award is presented as the Grand
    Prize for Best in Show in culinary art competition,
    1972, 1973

Citation from the United States Olympic Committee for
    distinguished service rendered to five Qlympiads, Winter
    Olympics, and Pan American Competitions, 1973

Recipient of Diplôme d'Honneur by the Vatel Club, New York
    for eminent service rendered to the profession, 1973

Recipient of Diplôme d'Honneur and Médaille from the Société
    des Cuisiniers de Paris for services rendered to the culinary
    profession, 1973

Recipient of the Key to New Orleans for participating as
    Judge for the Culinary Exhibit at the New Orleans Food
    Festival in June, 1973

Honored by the Culinary Brigade of The Greenbrier for
    having instituted the Greenbrier Culinary Apprentice
    Program and guiding all its scholars to a successful
    start in their careers, 1973

Appointed Honorary President of the Société Culinaire
    Philanthropique in April, 1974

Recipient of the West Virginia University Director's Award
    for contribution to National and International Olympics,
    1974

Recipient of the Silver Plate with the West Virginia Seal
    on behalf of Governor Arch A. Moore and the West Virginia
    Department of Commerce, 1974

Member of the Order of the Golden Toque, Culinary Institute
    of America, Hyde Park, New York, 1974

Recipient of the Educational Institute Award by the
    American Culinary Federation of America, 1974

APPETIZERS

Appetizers are small portions of food served before or at the beginning of a meal. In the United States, it has become customary to serve them with drinks, often in the living room. The main purpose of appetizers is to stimulate the taste buds, creating an anticipation for the food that is to follow. It is important, therefore, to choose appetizers that complement the entrée. For example, a highly seasoned appetizer can be served with a simple roast or fish entrée. On the other hand, if the main dish is complicated or spicy, one should serve a simpler appetizer with a flavor that does not conflict.

Although the appetizer with cocktails is something of an American tradition, recipes for these first courses come from all over the world, a fact that is reflected in the international character of the recipes I have chosen.

At The Greenbrier, appetizers fall into two categories: canapés, or finger sandwiches, and hors d'oeuvres. Many of the hors d'oeuvres can be used as luncheon or supper dishes.

19

This raw meat dish can be used in smaller portions for appetizers or in larger portions for a main luncheon course. Many Steak Tartare recipes call for ground meat; this one uses chopped meat.

STEAK TARTARE GREENBRIER

6 anchovy fillets

1 teaspoon olive oil

½ teaspoon salt

½ teaspoon pepper

1 medium-sized onion, peeled and finely chopped

½ teaspoon dry mustard

½ teaspoon paprika

1 teaspoon chopped, fresh tarragon leaves

1 teaspoon chopped, fresh parsley

1 teaspoon vinegar

1 teaspoon catsup

1 teaspoon lemon juice

1 teaspoon Worcestershire sauce

1 teaspoon drained capers

2 egg yolks, slightly beaten

*1 pound finely chopped beef
(lean sirloin or fillet)*

1 teaspoon brandy (optional)

In a bowl, crush the anchovy fillets with the oil. Add salt, pepper, onion, mustard, paprika, tarragon, parsley, vinegar, catsup, lemon juice, Worcestershire sauce, and capers. Blend well and stir in egg yolks. Add the raw beef and use your hands to knead meat well, thoroughly mixing in the sauce. Add brandy, if desired. For appetizers, spread mixture on wedges of toast. For a main course, reshape the meat into the form of a small steak, place it on lettuce leaves; garnish with sliced tomatoes, and serve with melba toast or rye bread. Serves four for main course or eight for appetizers.

The artichoke is a member of the thistle family and is one of the most easily digested vegetables. Legend places its origin in Africa, where it was the favorite of Anthony and Cleopatra.

ARTICHAUTS A LA ROMAINE
(ROMAN-STYLE ARTICHOKES)

8 medium-sized artichokes

1 lemon, cut in half

½ cup grated Parmesan cheese

½ cup fine, dry bread crumbs

1 tablespoon chopped chives

1 tablespoon chopped, fresh parsley

1 tablespoon chopped, peeled garlic

1 tablespoon chopped, peeled onion

1 tablespoon chopped green pepper

1 tablespoon chopped anchovy fillets

½ cup vegetable oil

1 garlic clove, peeled and crushed

1 bay leaf

½ teaspoon dried oregano

1 cup dry white wine

salt and pepper to taste

Wash artichokes well. Remove any bruised leaves. Cut off about 1 inch from tops of artichokes, and trim sharp tips from leaves with scissors. Cut a slice, approximately 1½ inches thick, from the bottom and scoop out the choke (thistle portion) from the center. Discard the choke. Rub cut surfaces with lemon. In a bowl, mix together Parmesan cheese, bread crumbs, chives, parsley, garlic, onion, green pepper, and anchovies. Fill the artichoke cavities with the mixture. Heat oil in a large saucepan (not aluminum). Add crushed garlic, bay leaf, and oregano. Place artichokes in the saucepan and sauté until golden brown on all sides. Add white wine, cover the pan, and let simmer gently for 45 minutes. Add salt and pepper to taste. Serve hot or cold. Serves eight.

This is a wonderful way to start a meal and a perfect recipe to perk up the taste buds. It's also a good way to use leftover meat.

SAUERKRAUT BALLS

½ *pound lean, boneless ham*

½ *pound lean, boneless pork*

½ *pound corned beef, cooked*

1 medium-sized onion, peeled and quartered

1 teaspoon chopped, fresh parsley

3 tablespoons shortening

2 cups all-purpose flour

1 teaspoon dry mustard

1 teaspoon salt

2 cups milk

2 pounds cooked, drained, finely chopped sauerkraut

2 eggs, slightly beaten

Put meats and onion through food grinder (or buy pre-ground). Add parsley, and blend well. Heat shortening in a large skillet, add meat mixture, and sauté until browned. Add flour, mustard, salt, milk, slightly beaten eggs, and sauerkraut; blend well. Cook over medium heat, stirring constantly, until thick. Cool and form into balls about the size of a walnut. Pour oil to a depth of 2 inches into a deep-fat fryer or heavy saucepan and heat to about 375°F. on a deep-frying thermometer. Fry sauerkraut balls, a few at a time, about 2 minutes, until browned. Drain on paper towels. Serve hot. Makes approximately 60 to 80 sauerkraut balls.

Traditionally a Swiss dish, fondue has gained popularity rapidly in the United States, and is often served as a light supper. Authentic fondue must be made with Gruyère cheese.

FONDUE AU FROMAGE SUISSE
(CHEESE FONDUE)

1 garlic clove, peeled, crushed, and chopped

2 cups dry white wine

1 pound Gruyère cheese, grated and chilled

1 teaspoon flour

¼ teaspoon each, salt, nutmeg, and pepper

2 tablespoons kirsch

1 loaf French bread

Rub a chafing dish with garlic, add wine and heat slowly over chafing dish burner. Shread cheese and lightly mix it with the flour. When the bubbles in the wine rise to the surface (do not boil), add the cheese mixture a handful at a time, stirring until each handful melts; continue until all cheese is added. Add seasoning and kirsch; stir well. Turn heat low, but keep fondue slowly bubbling. Cut French bread into cubes. Provide long-handled forks so that each guest may spear bread cubes and dip them in the fondue, with a stirring motion. If the fondue becomes too thick, add a little hot wine. Serves four.

ARTICHAUTS A LA GRECQUE
(GREEK ARTICHOKES)

6 medium-sized artichoke bottoms

1 lemon, cut in half

½ cup vegetable oil

¼ teaspoon each, salt and pepper

juice of 1 lemon

1 cup dry white wine

*1 bouquet garni (2 bay leaves, 2 sprigs
fresh parsley, 1 sprig fresh thyme)*

2 cloves

6 coriander seeds

6 peppercorns

1 lemon peel, thinly sliced

1 garlic clove, peeled and crushed

Remove outside leaves from artichokes, leaving only the bottom fleshy center portion. Scoop out the choke (thistle portion) and rub bottom with cut lemon. Cut each bottom into triangles. Heat oil in a large saucepan; add artichoke bottoms and salt and pepper, and sauté for two minutes. Add all other ingredients; cover and simmer for 30 minutes. When tender, remove artichoke bottoms and place on a serving dish. Reduce the liquid to half its volume over medium heat; strain and pour over artichoke bottoms. Serve hot or cold. Serves four.

The French feel that eggs, cheese, and bacon were created just for quiche. This is one of the more traditional and popular versions. This appetizer may be served hot or cold. It also makes an excellent light main course.

QUICHE LORRAINE

1 pastry shell, 9-inch size

3 eggs

2 cups light cream

½ cup grated, sharp cheese

1 tablespoon melted butter

¼ teaspoon each, salt, pepper, and nutmeg

pinch cayenne

4 slices bacon, minced

½ cup diced, cooked ham

½ cup peeled, chopped onions

½ cup diced Swiss cheese

Have baked pastry shell ready. Preheat oven to 350°F. In a bowl whip eggs and mix in cream, grated cheese, butter, salt, pepper, nutmeg, and cayenne. In a skillet, sauté bacon, ham, and onions until the onions are transparent. Spread onion mixture evenly on the bottom of the pastry shell. Sprinkle with diced Swiss cheese. Fill to rim of shell with the egg mixture and bake at 350°F. for 25 minutes or until center is set. Serves eight.

VIANDE DE CRABE BONNE FEMME
(CRABMEAT WITH MUSHROOMS)

2 tablespoons butter

1 pound cleaned crabmeat

¼ pound mushrooms, diced

2 tablespoons brandy

¼ teaspoon each, salt and pepper

juice of ½ lemon

*2 cups White Wine and Fish Sauce
(see index), heated*

2 egg yolks, slightly beaten

½ cup heavy cream

3 tablespoons grated, sharp cheese

Melt butter in a large saucepan; add crabmeat, diced mushrooms, brandy, salt, pepper, and lemon juice. Pour in heated White Wine and Fish Sauce, and simmer gently, uncovered, 30 minutes. Combine egg yolks and cream, and add 1/3 of the mixture to the crabmeat. Pour crabmeat mixture into buttered 1½ quart baking dish. Top with rest of egg yolk mixture, sprinkle grated cheese over top, and place in pre-heated broiler three inches from heat until golden brown (3 to 4 minutes). Serves three.

This canapé spread is proof of the adage "sherry to stew, brandy to finish." This spread is excellent on melba toast or crackers.

PUREE DE FOIE DE VOLAILLE
(BRANDIED CHICKEN LIVERS)

3 small onions, peeled and chopped

2 tablespoons butter

1 pound chicken livers

2/3 cup dry sherry

3 tablespoons brandy

salt and pepper to taste

Sauté onions in butter until golden. Add the chicken livers and sherry. Cover and simmer for 30 minutes. Put mixture through food grinder and then press through a sieve or purée the mixture in an electric blender. Add the brandy and the salt and pepper. It is important to add the brandy and the seasonings after the cooking. The sherry and brandy combine to take some of the sharp taste from the cooked chicken livers. Serves eight.

PALOURDES FARCIES
(STUFFED CLAMS)

½ cup butter

2 tablespoons peeled, chopped shallots

1 garlic clove, peeled, crushed, and chopped

1 tablespoon curry powder

1 tablespoon diced, peeled apple

1 tablespoon chopped chutney

½ cup dry white wine

½ cup heavy cream

½ cup White Wine and Fish Sauce (see index)

*2 dozen shucked clams, chopped
(reserve the juice and 24 half-shells)*

*¼ teaspoon each, salt, pepper,
and cayenne pepper*

½ cup toasted coconut

1 tablespoon chopped fresh parsley

Discard any clams that are not tightly closed. Preheat oven to 375°F. Heat ¼ cup of the butter in a 4-quart saucepan, and sauté the garlic and shallots until golden brown. Add the curry powder, apples, and chutney. When well-heated, add the wine and reserved clam juice over medium heat. Reduce to two-thirds its volume. Add cream, White Wine and Fish Sauce, and bring to a boil. Add the chopped clams to the mixture, and season with salt, pepper, and cayenne. Simmer for 5 minutes; cool. Fill 24 clam shells with the mixture, and sprinkle with toasted coconut. Top with the remaining ¼-cup melted butter. Bake at 375°F. for 5 minutes. Place 6 clams on each plate and garnish with chopped parsley. Serves four.

Mussels, an old Indian seafood that was greatly neglected until a decade ago, are found in great masses along both coasts.

MOULES A L'INDIENNE
(CURRIED MUSSELS)

2 quarts mussels

1 cup dry white wine

½ cup onions, peeled and chopped

1 teaspoon dried thyme

1 bay leaf

¼ teaspoon salt

¼ teaspoon pepper

1 tablespoon curry powder

1 cup mayonnaise

½ cup sour cream

½ cup shredded coconut

Discard any mussels that are not tightly closed. Scrub well under cold, running water. With a sharp knife, trim off the beard around the edges. Cook mussels in a 4-quart saucepan with wine, onions, thyme, bay leaf, salt, and pepper until they open. Remove from heat and remove mussels from pan. Discard bay leaf. Over medium heat, reduce liquid to one-third its volume. Add curry powder, mayonnaise, and sour cream; mix well. Each mussel has two shells; snap these apart and discard empty half-shell. Cut mussel away from remaining half-shell and remove sandbag. Then return each mussel to half-shell, and top with some of the curry sauce mixture. Arrange mussels on serving dishes (six per serving) and sprinkle with coconut. Serves four.

GUACAMOLE

2 ripe avocados, peeled and mashed

1 tablespoon peeled, chopped onion

1 small garlic clove, peeled,
crushed, and chopped

1 tablespoon peeled, seeded,
and chopped tomato

1 tablespoon catsup

½ teaspoon prepared horseradish

1 dash Tabasco sauce

juice of one lemon

salt and pepper to taste

Combine all ingredients and press mixture through a fine sieve. Serve with Fritos. Serves eight.

Canapé is a French word meaning sofa, couch, or divan that gradually became a culinary term. Canapés are simply hors d'oeuvres served on bread cut into small, fancy shapes. Canapés are made to eat with the fingers.

CANAPES

Use thin slices of bread. Remove crusts and cut in different shapes, such as rounds, squares, triangles, diamonds, hearts or strips. Sauté pieces in butter on both sides and cover with one of the mixtures below:

CREAM CHEESE SPREAD Moisten 8 ounces of cream cheese with 2 tablespoons cream.

AVOCADO SPREAD Season 1 large avocado, peeled and mashed, with 2 tablespoons lemon juice and ½ teaspoon salt.

TUNA SPREAD Mix 1 can (about 7 ounces) tuna, drained and flaked, with 2 tablespoons lemon juice, 2 tablespoons grated onion and ¼ cup mayonnaise.

CHICKEN SPREAD Mix 1 cup finely chopped cooked chicken with 4 hard-cooked eggs (chopped) and ¼ cup minced sautéed onion. Moisten with ¼ cup mayonnaise.

CAVIAR Spread caviar on buttered canapé base.

SARDINE Place whole sardine on buttered base, sprinkle with finely chopped onions.

HERRING Place square cut of herring fillet on base and garnish with small slice of dill pickle.

SHRIMP Cover base with mayonnaise and top with one-half cooked shrimp. Garnish with a slice of stuffed olive.

HAM Cover base with prepared mustard and top with a thin slice of ham. Decorate with an asparagus tip.

SALAMI Spread liverwurst on base and top with slice of salami.

SWISS CHEESE Cover base with prepared mustard and top with a slice of Swiss cheese. Garnish with radish slices.

BOHEMIAN Pumpernickel bread may be substituted for usual canapé base. Spread bread with canned deviled ham and decorate with sliced gherkins.

ROSE MARIE Spread cream cheese on brown bread and garnish with radish and gherkin slices.

TAHITIAN Substitute pumpernickel bread. Spread pimento cheese between two slices of pumpernickel. Slice in ½ inch-wide fingers and sprinkle with chopped, toasted coconut.

STOCKS

Stocks are the mainstay of elegant cuisine. A stock is a broth made from meat, poultry, fish, game, or vegetables. Meat, poultry, bones, fish trimmings are simmered with water to which have been added spices and seasonings, which vary depending upon the recipe.

Although stocks are easy to prepare, they require long hours of cooking. Only proper ingredients and ample cooking time will produce a flavorful stock. Because of the great amount of cooking time involved, rather large quantities have been suggested. If you freeze the stock in small containers, future sauces and soups will be that much easier to prepare. If you prefer to make a smaller quantity, cut the recipe in half.

Stocks fall into seven categories: brown stock, which is made from meat; white stock, which is generally made from veal and a combination of other meat; chicken stock; game stock; vegetable stock, probably the most delicate of the stocks; fish stock, also very delicate; and meat glaze, which is a form of reduced stock that is used to coat meat while it is cooking.

Many stocks are seasoned with a bouquet garni. Unless otherwise stated in a recipe, a bouquet garni consists of two sprigs of parsley, one sprig of thyme, and one bay leaf, all neatly tied up in cheesecloth.

As a general rule, stocks should be simmered, or cooked just below the boiling point, rather than boiled. When the ingredients have been added to the water in the kettle, the mixture should be brought to a rolling boil; then the heat should be reduced to a simmer.

If you are pressed for time, you may substitute any one of the canned products available, such as chicken broth or beef broth or bouillon. Some gourmet shops sell fish stock, or you may use clam broth. Meat glaze can be replaced with Kitchen Bouquet. You should use a substitute only as a last resort, however, because one can never adequately substitute quality for availability.

This stock will be clear and of good flavor and can be served as a broth or used as a base for sauces.

FOND BRUN
(BROWN STOCK)

2 pounds beef short ribs

2 pounds veal knuckles (or shank)

4 pounds beef bones

2 carrots, scraped

2 stalks celery

1 onion, peeled

10 peppercorns, crushed

1 bouquet garni (1 bay leaf, 2 sprigs fresh parsley, 1 sprig fresh thyme)

4 tomatoes

1 garlic clove, peeled

1 tablespoon salt

Preheat oven to 425°F. Cut up ribs and veal knuckles in large pieces (or have your butcher do this); spread them in a large flat roasting pan with the beef bones, and roast at 425°F. for 15 minutes. Add carrots, celery, onion, and peppercorns; roast another 15 minutes. Transfer everything from the roasting pan to an 8-quart kettle. Add 6 quarts of water, the bouquet garni, tomatoes, garlic, and salt. Bring very slowly to a boil. Remove any scum from the top with a spoon. Cover and simmer (do not boil) over low heat for 4 hours. Cool. Skim the fat from the top, and strain the whole mixture through a sieve and then through cheesecloth. Yields four quarts.

This mild stock is used for diet soups and white sauces.

FOND BLANC
(WHITE STOCK)

1 four-pound chicken, cut into quarters

4 pounds veal shoulder with bone

1 veal knuckle

2 carrots, scraped

2 stalks celery

1 onion, peeled

10 peppercorns, crushed

*1 bouquet garni (1 bay leaf, 2 sprigs parsley,
1 sprig thyme)*

1 garlic clove

1 tablespoon salt

Parboil the chicken for 40 minutes. Preheat oven to 425°F. Cut up veal shoulder and veal knuckle in large pieces. Spread in a large flat roasting pan and roast at 425°F. for 15 minutes. Add carrots, celery, onion, and peppercorns, and roast another 15 minutes. Transfer everything from roasting pan to an 8-quart kettle. Add the chicken, 6 quarts of water, the bouquet garni, garlic, and salt. Bring very slowly to a boil. Remove any scum from top with a spoon. Cover and let simmer over low heat for 4 hours. Cool. Skim the fat from the top; strain the whole mixture through a sieve and then through cheesecloth. Yields four quarts.

This may be served garnished with rice and diced fowl.

FOND DE VOLAILLE
(CHICKEN BROTH)

2 four-pound chickens, cut in quarters

1 veal knuckle

5 pounds chicken backs, necks, and wings

2 carrots, scraped

2 stalks celery

1 onion, peeled

10 peppercorns

*1 bouquet garni (1 bay leaf, 2 sprigs parsley,
1 sprig thyme)*

1 garlic clove, peeled

1 tablespoon salt

Parboil the chickens. Preheat oven to 425°F. Cut up veal knuckle in large pieces; spread in a large flat roasting pan, and roast at 425°F. for 15 minutes. Add carrots, celery, onion, and peppercorns; let roast for another 15 minutes. Transfer everything from roasting pan to an 8-quart kettle. Add all the chicken, 6 quarts of water, the bouquet garni, garlic, and salt. Bring very slowly to a boil. Remove any scum from top with a spoon. Cover and let simmer (do not boil) over low heat for 4 hours. Cool. Skim the fat from the top; strain the whole mixture through a sieve, and then through cheesecloth. Yields four quarts.

FOND DE LEGUMES
(VEGETABLE STOCK)

2 quarts water

2 carrots, scraped

2 onions, peeled

2 stalks celery

2 leeks, cleaned

½ head cabbage, chopped

2 whole tomatoes

10 peppercorns

1 garlic clove, peeled

1 tablespoon salt

*1 bouquet garni (1 bay leaf, 2 sprigs parsley,
1 sprig thyme)*

Combine all ingredients in a large kettle, and bring to a boil. Cover and simmer for 1 hour. Strain the broth through cheesecloth. If not needed immediately, stock may be stored in glass jars in the refrigerator for several days. Yields 1¾ quarts.

This stock is used for clear, cream, puréed and compound soups and also for gravies. A compound soup is two soups together; i.e., pea and turtle make Boula-Boula . . .

FUMET DE GIBIER
(GAME STOCK)

5 pounds bones and trimmings of any game

1 veal shank, cut in pieces

2 carrots, scraped

2 stalks celery

2 onions, peeled

2 garlic cloves, peeled

10 peppercorns

10 juniper berries

4 whole tomatoes

1 bouquet garni (1 bay leaf, 1 sprig parsley,
1 sprig thyme)

1 tablespoon salt

Preheat oven to 425°F. Spread game bones and trimmings and veal shank pieces in large flat roasting pan, and roast for 15 minutes. Add carrots, celery, onions, garlic, peppercorns, and juniper berries; roast another 10 minutes. Transfer everything from roasting pan to an 8-quart kettle. Add 6 quarts water, tomatoes, bouquet garni, and salt. Bring very slowly to a boil. Remove any scum from top with a spoon. Cover and let simmer over low heat for 4 hours. Cool. Skim the fat from the top; strain the whole mixture through a sieve, and then through cheesecloth. Yields four quarts.

This is a light, flavorful broth to use in soups, sauces, and seafood dishes.

FUMET DE POISSON
(FISH STOCK)

2 pounds bones and trimmings from fresh fish

2 onions, peeled and sliced

2 stalks celery

10 peppercorns

2 garlic cloves, peeled

*1 bouquet garni (1 bay leaf, 2 sprigs parsley,
1 sprig thyme)*

½ cup peeled, chopped shallots

½ cup butter

1 cup dry white wine

Place bones and fish trimmings, onions, celery, peppercorns, garlic, bouquet garni, and 2 quarts water in a large saucepan. Slowly bring to a boil. Remove scum from top with a spoon. Cover and let simmer for 30 minutes. Cool. Strain mixture through cheesecloth into a clean saucepan. Sauté the shallots in the butter in a skillet until golden brown. Add shallots and the wine to the strained stock. Bring quickly to a boil and reduce liquid to 1 quart over medium heat. Yields one quart.

This is a reduced meat stock that is used to glaze meats. It can also be used in sauces.

LA GLACE DE VIANDE
(MEAT GLAZE)

To make a glaze, put the bones and vegetables from any of the preceding stocks back into a kettle; add enough water to completely cover the ingredients, and let simmer for 3 hours. Strain the mixture through cheesecloth into a saucepan, and return to the stove over low heat. Reduce slowly to a heavy syrup. Strain again into a smaller saucepan. Reduce over *very* low heat, until the substance has the consistency of marmalade. Pour into a container and store in a refrigerator or freezer.

SOUPS

Soup requires more attention than many people care to give it, but adequate attention gives worthwhile results. Even before your guests sit down to dinner, they will be tantalized by the aroma of good soup drifting from your kitchen.

Canned soup is all right for those in a hurry, but if you want a fine aroma and flavor, you must make your own. Sometimes I close my eyes and I recall my mother's cooking. I always smell her soups first. I can see her returning from the market with a basket of fish trimmings and beef bones, gathering the spices, and chopping the vegetables to go into the soup. And I remember most particularly the aroma of the soup as it bubbled on the stove.

The old-fashioned aroma of homemade soup is returning. Many people are growing their own spices, herbs, and vegetables. Homemade soup can't be far behind.

A delightful and unusual soup that makes an excellent first course.

MULLIGATAWNY SOUP

½ cup peeled, diced apple

½ cup diced, peeled eggplant

3 tablespoons butter

½ cup peeled, chopped onions

½ cup chopped celery

½ cup all-purpose flour

4 tablespoons curry powder

½ cup tomato purée

1½ quarts Brown Stock (see index)

½ cup heavy cream

salt and pepper to taste

Preheat oven to 375°F. Sauté apples and eggplant in 1½ tablespoons of the butter for 5 minutes, and set aside. In a skillet with an ovenproof handle, sauté onions and celery in the remaining 1½ tablespoons butter until golden brown. Stir in flour and curry powder and bake at 375°F. for 10 minutes. Put onion and celery mixture into a large saucepan. Add the tomato purée and Brown Stock and bring to a boil. Cover and simmer for 30 minutes. Strain soup through a sieve, and put liquid back in saucepan. Bring to a boil and add the cream and sautéed apples and eggplant. Add salt and pepper to taste.

Note: This soup may also be served cold with added cream (½ cup). It is then called Senegalese Soup. Serves eight.

This soup is delicious served hot or cold. This unusual version is well worth the effort it takes.

BORSCHT
(RUSSIAN BEET SOUP)

6 medium-sized beets, scrubbed, julienned, and cooked in 2 cups water with 1 tablespoon vinegar

2 leeks, washed and julienned

2 stalks celery, julienned

1 onion, peeled and chopped

3 sprigs fresh parsley

2 tablespoons butter

1½ quarts Brown Stock (see index)

1 three-pound duck, roasted in 325°F. oven about 1¼ hours

1 pound beef round, simmered in a little water for 1 hour

¼ head cabbage, diced

1 spice bag with 1 bay leaf, 2 cloves, 2 sprigs fresh marjoram

½ cup beet juice (saved from cooking beets)

salt and pepper to taste

6 tablespoons sour cream (to garnish cold soup)

Reserve the water in which the beets were cooked. In a large kettle, sauté beets, leeks, celery, onion, and parsley in the butter for 15 minutes. Add Brown Stock, duck, beef, cabbage, and spice bag. Cover and simmer for 1 hour. Remove the duck, beef ribs, and spice bag. Skim fat from the surface. Cut the breasts of the duck and the beef from the ribs into small squares and add to the soup. Bring to a boil again, and add the reserved beet juice. Add salt and pepper to taste. Place a tablespoonful of sour cream on top of each serving, if soup is cold. Serves six.

This cold soup, a great Spanish contribution, is actually a thick, spicy tomato soup.

GAZPACHO

4 cups peeled, diced tomatoes

1½ cups chopped, seeded green pepper

¾ cup peeled, chopped onion

1 garlic clove, peeled and minced

2 cups canned beef bouillon

½ cup lemon juice

¼ cup olive oil

1 tablespoon paprika

2 teaspoons salt

¼ teaspoon pepper

½ cup thinly sliced cucumber

Purée all ingredients except the cucumber in an electric blender. Let stand at room temperature for 1 hour, stirring frequently. Chill for at least 2 hours. Add cucumbers just before serving. Serves six.

This soup is a chilled variation of potato soup—and an elegant start for any dinner.

VICHYSSOISE

¼ *cup sliced, peeled onions*

2 *tablespoons butter*

2 *cups thinly sliced, peeled potatoes*

2 *cups Chicken Broth (see index)*

1½ *teaspoons salt*

1½ *cups milk*

1 *cup heavy cream*

*Worcestershire and Tabasco sauce,
celery salt to taste*

2 *tablespoons chopped chives*

In a large saucepan, sauté onions in the butter until tender. Add potatoes, Chicken Broth, and salt; bring to a boil. Cover and simmer for 30 minutes. Press mixture through a fine sieve or purée in an electric blender. Add milk; bring to a boil. Remove from heat and cool. Add cream, Worcestershire sauce, Tabasco sauce, and celery salt to taste. Chill. Serve very cold garnished with chives. Additional zest may be obtained by adding about one tablespoon finely minced green onion when cream is added. Serves six.

This hearty soup, heavy with onion, bread, and cheese, can easily serve as a meal in itself.

SOUPE A L'OIGNON
(FRENCH ONION SOUP)

½ cup butter

3 large onions, peeled and sliced

1½ quarts Chicken Broth (see index)

1 cup dry white wine

¼ teaspoon salt

¼ teaspoon pepper

4 slices French bread, toasted

1 cup grated Gruyère cheese

Preheat oven to 400°F. Melt butter in a large saucepan, and sauté the onions until golden brown. Add Chicken Broth gradually, and simmer slowly for 20 minutes. Add white wine and salt and pepper. Pour soup into 4-quart ovenproof casserole. Place slices of bread on top, and sprinkle with cheese. Set casserole in a pan of hot water and bake at 1400°F. for 10 minutes. Serves six.

Régime soup has very little seasoning and is sometimes prescribed by doctors as part of a bland diet.

SOUPE DE REGIME
(DIET SOUP)

½ cup butter

½ cup flour

2 cups rolled oats

½ cup cold water

3 quarts White Stock (see index)

3 cups milk

liaison of 1 cup heavy cream and 3 egg yolks beaten together (optional)

Melt butter in a large saucepan; add flour, stir, and cook slowly until golden in color. Then add rolled oats and cook gently for 5 minutes. Add water to cut heat, and then, gradually stir in White Stock. Bring to a boil, and let simmer for 1 hour. Strain soup through a fine sieve; add milk, and reheat to boiling point. If adding liaison, mix some of the soup into it to warm it before adding to the mixture. For variation, rice or barley may be used in place of rolled oats. Use same amount, but let the soup simmer for 2 hours. Sugar may also be added, to taste.

Most puréed soups are made from légumes, such as split peas, navy beans, and lentils. The vegetables form a liaison as they cook, and it is not necessary to bind them with cream and/or eggs. It used to be a rule to soak these vegetables overnight and cook them for many hours. Today, this is not always necessary. Split peas, for example, are merely rinsed and added to a kettle of water; in two or three hours, you can have Potage St. Germain.

POTAGE ST. GERMAIN
(SPLIT PEA SOUP)

½ pound green split peas

½ cup butter

1 stalk celery, diced

1 leek, washed and diced

1 onion, peeled and diced

2 potatoes, peeled and diced

1 ham bone or 2 ham hocks

2 quarts water

¼ teaspoon salt

¼ teaspoon pepper

1 cup toasted bread croutons

Follow directions on package for preparing peas. Drain. Heat butter in a large saucepan and sauté celery, leek, onion, and potatoes for 10 minutes over medium heat. Add the split peas, ham bone or hocks, and water. Simmer covered for 1½ hours or until peas are tender. Discard the bone and purée liquid in an electric blender (or press through a fine sieve). Return soup to saucepan and bring to a boil. Add salt and pepper. Serve with bread croutons. Serves six to eight.

VARIATIONS

POTAGE LONGCHAMPS

(Split Pea Soup with Vermicelli)

Follow the directons for split pea soup, but add Chinese vermicelli to replace the bread croutons as garniture.

POTAGE LAMBALLE

(Split Pea Soup with Tapioca)

Follow the directions for split pea soup, but add ¼ cup prepared quick-cooking tapioca and omit the bread croutons.

POTAGE DE LENTILLES

(Lentil Soup)

Follow the same procedure as for split pea soup, but add ½ pound dried lentils instead of the split peas. Sliced cooked sausages may be added as garnish.

POTAGE SOISSONS

(Navy Bean Soup)

Follow the directions for split pea soup, but use dried navy beans to replace split peas. Garnish with ¼ cup diced cooked carrots, leeks, celery, or onions.

This is a favorite in the French Quarter of New Orleans.

BISQUE DE HOMARD
(LOBSTER SOUP)

4 tablespoons butter

½ cup peeled, diced onion

1 stalk celery, diced

1 sprig fresh parsley

2 tomatoes, peeled and diced

1 sprig fresh thyme

2 large, frozen lobster tails, thawed

¼ teaspoon each, salt, pepper, paprika

¼ cup brandy

¾ cup dry white wine

½ cup all-purpose flour

½ cup tomato purée

1½ quarts White Wine and Fish Sauce (see index)

2 egg yolks

1 cup heavy cream

Heat 2 tablespoons of the butter in a large saucepan; add onion, celery, parsley, tomatoes, and thyme, and sauté slowly until tender. (This mixture is called a *mirepoix.*) Add lobster tails and sauté them until the shells are quite red. Add salt, pepper, and paprika. Pour on brandy and white wine and ignite. When flame dies down, add flour and tomato purée and mix well. Gradually add White Wine and Fish Sauce. Bring to a boil and let simmer over low heat for 30 minutes. Remove lobster tails, reserving the meat. Dice the meat and reserve it for garnish. Pound lobster shells with a meat mallet and add to soup. Let simmer another 30 minutes. Strain mixture through a sieve into a glass bowl, and then through cheesecloth. Return to the saucepan and bring to a boil. Lightly beat the egg yolks and cream. Slowly add the mixture to the soup; mix well, and remove from heat. Add the remaining 2 tablespoons butter. Garnish the soup with diced lobster. Serves eight.

ESSENCE DE PALOURDES
(CLAM BROTH)

4 dozen clams

1½ quarts water

1 teaspoon celery salt

Scrub clam shells, and wash several times until free from sand. Place clams in a large kettle. Add water and celery salt. Cover tightly and cook slowly over low heat for 20 minutes or until shells open (but not *less* than 20 minutes). Remove clams from broth, being careful to keep all liquid in kettle. Serve clams on half-shell, or remove from shells and use as desired. Strain clam liquor (liquid) carefully through a cheesecloth, and serve hot or cold. Serves four.

VARIATIONS

CLAM BROTH BELLEVUE I

Use one part clam broth and one part turtle soup (canned or fresh). Top with whipped cream.

CLAM BROTH BELLEVUE II

Use one part clam broth to one part beef consommé. Top with whipped cream.

CLAM BROTH BON VIVANTS

Use clam broth with clams (thoroughly desanded and cleaned) served in a soup bowl with one teaspoon of butter and ½ teaspoon chopped, fresh parsley added to each bowl.

Instead of cream you may finish these soups with a liaison made of two egg yolks and one cup of cream.

CREAM OF LETTUCE SOUP

½ cup butter

1 large onion, peeled and chopped

1 garlic clove, peeled, crushed, and chopped

½ cup all-purpose flour

*1½ quarts Chicken Broth (see index),
heated to lukewarm*

1 pound blanched, chopped lettuce

2 cups half-and-half cream

salt and pepper to taste

½ cup shredded green lettuce

2½ tablespoons butter

Melt the ½ cup butter in a 4-quart saucepan; add onion and garlic, and sauté until golden brown. Add flour and mix well. Gradually stir in warm Chicken Broth and let it come to a boil. Add blanched lettuce, cover and simmer for 50 minutes. Remove from heat and press through a fine sieve or purée in an electric blender. Return soup to saucepan and bring to a boil; add cream. Add salt and pepper to taste. In a small skillet, sauté shredded lettuce in the 2½ tablespoons butter until wilted in appearance. Top each serving of soup with lettuce and butter mixture. Serves six.

VARIATIONS

POTAGE LAVALLIERE

(Cream of Celery)

Follow the same procedure and use the same ingredients as for cream of lettuce soup, except replace the blanched lettuce leaves with eight stalks of celery (including leaves) coarsely chopped. Garnish with one tablespoon diced celery simmered in a little Chicken Broth.

DUBARRY

(Cream of Cauliflower)

Follow the same procedure and use the same ingredients as for cream of lettuce soup, except replace the blanched lettuce leaves with one pound of fresh cauliflower coarsely cut up. Garnish with small pieces of cauliflower that have been simmered in a little Chicken Broth for about 20 minutes.

CRECY

(Cream of Carrot)

Follow the same procedure and use the same ingredients as for cream of lettuce soup, except replace the blanched lettuce leaves with one pound sliced, scraped carrots and ½ pound cubed, peeled potatoes. Garnish with small bread croutons.

CRECY AUX PERLES DU JAPON

Garnish cream of carrot soup with ¼ cup quick-cooking tapioca pearls that have been poached in water until clear.

CRECY AU RIZ

Garnish cream of carrot soup with ¼ cup pre-cooked rice.

DORIA

(Cream of Cucumber)

Follow the same procedure and use the same ingredients as for cream of lettuce soup, except replace the blanched lettuce leaves with one pound thickly sliced cucumbers. Garnish with chopped cucumbers.

CREME DE VOLAILLES
(CREAM OF CHICKEN)

½ cup butter

½ cup all-purpose flour

*¾ quart Chicken Broth (see index),
heated to lukewarm*

½ cup heavy cream

1 breast of chicken, poached and diced

Melt butter in a saucepan; add flour and cook over medium heat 5 minutes. Gradually add Chicken Broth and bring to a boil. Cover and simmer 1 hour. Remove from heat and strain through a fine sieve. Return soup to saucepan and bring to a boil. Add cream. Garnish with diced cooked chicken breast. Serves four.

VELOUTE DE TOMATES
(CREAM OF TOMATO)

3 tablespoons butter

1 onion, peeled and chopped

1 stalk celery, chopped

1 garlic clove, peeled, crushed, and chopped

1 tablespoon flour

½ teaspoon dried thyme leaves

¼ teaspoon black pepper

¼ teaspoon salt

6 ripe tomatoes, coarsely chopped

1 cup tomato purée

2 cups Brown Stock (see index)

*liaison of ½ cup heavy cream, 1 egg yolk,
beaten together*

Melt 2 tablespoons of the butter in a saucepan; add onion, celery and garlic, and sauté 10 minutes. Add flour, mix well. Add thyme, pepper, salt, tomatoes, tomato purée, and Brown Stock. Cover and cook slowly for 1½ hours. Remove from heat and strain through a sieve or purée in an electric blender. Return soup to saucepan and bring to a boil. Fold in the liaison, and add remaining 1 tablespoon butter. Serves four.

1856 - 1922

HERE STOOD A FAMOUS HOSTELRY
AFFECTIONATELY KNOWN AS

THE · OLD · WHITE

ONCE THE PRIDE OF THE OLD DOMINION

WHOSE GRACIOUS HOSPITALITY, BEAUTIFUL
SURROUNDINGS AND HEALING WATERS GAINED
NATIONAL RENOWN AND MADE IT THE OBJECT
OF MANY A PILGRIMAGE.

HERE GATHERED FROM THE NORTH AND SOUTH
GREAT GENERALS, FAMOUS STATESMEN AND
PHILANTHROPISTS, LOVELY LADIES AND
REIGNING BELLES "WHO LEFT UPON THE SILENT
SHORE OF MEMORY" IMAGES AND PRECIOUS
THOUGHTS THAT SHALL NOT DIE, AND
CANNOT BE DESTROYED".

ERECTED BY ITS SUCCESSOR

THE GREENBRIER

1940

SAUCES

Sauces are meant to enhance, never to smother the flavors of a food. Many sauces from French *haut cuisine,* classic in their ingredients and flavors, are still called by their original names— as *hollandaise* or *béarnaise,* which are intended to be used on vegetables and meat, respectively. In most cases, I have specified how a sauce can be used and what particular foods it enhances. Do not be afraid, however, to experiment with sauces on other foods, if you think an interesting flavor combination can be made.

Basically, a sauce is a combination of liquid (often a stock), seasoning, and a *liaison,* which binds everything together and thickens it.

There are several kinds of thickening agents used in vegetable, meat, and fish sauces: cornstarch, which makes a clear, delicate sauce; a *liaison* of eggs and cream, which makes a thick, rich sauce; *roux,* a combination of flour and melted butter, which makes a sauce with body; and egg whites, which make a fluffy sauce.

This is a basic sauce for which you will find many uses, particularly in finishing poultry and meat dishes.

SAUCE DEMI-GLACE
(BROWN SAUCE)

½ cup bacon fat

½ cup ham fat trimmings

1 large onion, peeled and chopped

3 carrots, scraped and chopped

4 stalks celery, chopped

2 leeks, cleaned and chopped

1 garlic clove, peeled and crushed

2 bay leaves

2 sprigs fresh parsley

1 teaspoon dried thyme leaves

½ cup all-purpose flour

½ cup dry white wine

½ cup tomato purée

2 quarts Brown Stock (see index)

salt and pepper to taste

Preheat oven to 375°F. Melt bacon fat with ham trimmings in a skillet with an ovenproof handle. Add onion, carrots, celery, leeks, garlic, bay leaves, parsley, and thyme. Cook over medium heat for 15 minutes, or until vegetables are lightly browned. Add flour, mix well and bake at 375°F. for a few minutes until flour is brown. Remove from oven and transfer mixture to a large kettle. Add wine, tomato purée, and Brown Stock. Cover and let simmer over low heat for 2 hours. Occasionally remove scum from top with a spoon. Strain sauce through a cheesecloth, and cool. Add salt and pepper to taste. Store in glass jars in refrigerator.

Served often with grilled meat or fish, fried fish, and other dishes.

MAITRE D'HOTEL

¼ *cup soft butter*

1 tablespoon lemon juice

1 tablespoon chopped parsley

1 tablespoon minced chives

½ *teaspoon salt*

¼ *teaspoon pepper*

Blend all ingredients thoroughly with a wooden spoon until smooth. Yields 1/3 cup.

This sauce is made from wine from the island of Madeira. If you can't find shallots, you can substitute green onions, but it isn't quite the same sauce.

SAUCE AU MADERE
(MADEIRA WINE SAUCE)

1 cup Madeira

½ *cup peeled and chopped shallots*

2 cups Sauce Demi-glace (see index)

2 tablespoons butter

In a saucepan combine Madeira and shallots. Cook over medium heat until wine is reduced to half its volume. Add Sauce Demi-glace, bring mixture to a boil, and simmer over low heat for 5 minutes. Strain sauce through a fine sieve, and add butter while sauce is still hot.

SAUCE BORDELAISE
(BORDELAISE SAUCE)

½ cup butter

½ cup peeled and chopped shallots

8 peppercorns, crushed

1 bay leaf

1 cup Bordeaux wine

2 cups Sauce Demi-glace (see index)

juice of ½ lemon

2 tablespoons butter

½ cup poached, diced bone marrow

Melt ½ cup butter in a saucepan. Add shallots, peppercorns, and bay leaf. Cook for 2 minutes over medium heat. Add wine, bring to a boil, and cook until wine is reduced to half its volume. Add Sauce Demi-glace and simmer for 10 minutes. Strain sauce through a fine sieve. Return mixture to saucepan and add lemon juice and 2 tablespoons butter. Keep warm. Add poached marrow when ready to serve.

The Marquis Louis de Béchamel, the great French financier and gastronome, is said to have invented this sauce, which has many uses and variations.

SAUCE BECHAMEL
(MILK SAUCE)

½ cup butter

½ cup all-purpose flour

1 quart milk, heated to lukewarm

1 tablespoon salt

½ teaspoon nutmeg

Melt butter in a saucepan; stir in flour and cook over low heat for 5 minutes or until flour begins to turn golden. Gradually add the milk, stirring constantly with a wire whip. Bring mixture to a boil, add salt and nutmeg, and cook over a low heat for 30 minutes, stirring frequently. Strain sauce through a fine sieve and cool. Store in glass jars in refrigerator and use as needed. Yields 1 quart.

Sauce Mornay is basically a béchamel sauce with cheese added. It is delicious served on egg and vegetable dishes.

SAUCE MORNAY

2 cups Béchamel Sauce (see index)

4 egg yolks

½ cup heavy cream

½ cup grated sharp cheese

¼ teaspoon each, salt, pepper and nutmeg

In a saucepan, heat Béchamel Sauce over low heat. In a bowl, beat egg yolks with cream and stir in a little of the hot Béchamel Sauce. Mix well. Stir the egg mixture into the remaining Béchamel Sauce. Let simmer gently for 3 minutes. Mix in the cheese; when cheese has melted, season with salt, pepper, and nutmeg and remove sauce from the heat. Yields 1 quart.

A delicate sauce that will enhance most fish dishes.

VELOUTE DE POISSON
(WHITE WINE AND FISH SAUCE)

½ cup butter

1 carrot, scraped and diced

1 onion, peeled and diced

1 stalk celery, diced

½ cup mushroom stems, coarsely chopped

1 garlic clove, peeled and chopped

10 peppercorns, crushed

2/3 cup all-purpose flour

1 cup dry white wine

*1 quart Fish Stock (see index),
heated to lukewarm*

Melt butter in a saucepan. Add carrot, onion, celery, mushroom stems, garlic, and peppercorns. Cook for 5 minutes. Add flour and simmer until flour starts to brown. Stir in wine and Fish Stock, whipping continuously until sauce is smooth. Bring to a boil and simmer for 30 minutes. Strain sauce through a fine sieve and cool. Store in jars in the refrigerator until needed.

The Lyonnais district of France produces fine onions, so it is only proper that this onion sauce be named after it. This is an excellent sauce on vegetables.

SAUCE LYONNAISE
(ONION SAUCE)

1/3 cup butter

2 large onions, peeled and coarsely chopped

½ cup dry white wine

2 tablespoons vinegar

2 cups Brown Sauce (see index)

juice of one lemon

salt and pepper to taste

Melt butter in a saucepan. Add onions and cook over medium heat until golden brown. Add wine and vinegar, and reduce mixture to half its volume over medium heat. Add Brown Sauce; bring to a boil, and simmer for 15 minutes. Add lemon juice and salt and pepper to taste. Yields 3 cups.

This basic sauce is used for many poultry and meat dishes. Its variations may be used in the same way.

SAUCE VELOUTE

½ cup butter

1 onion, peeled and diced

1 carrot, scraped and diced

1 stalk celery, diced

1 garlic clove, peeled and crushed

½ cup mushroom stems, coarsely chopped

10 peppercorns, crushed

2/3 cup all-purpose flour

*1 quart White Stock (see index),
heated to lukewarm*

1 cup heavy cream

3 egg yolks

½ cup dry white wine

¼ teaspoons each salt, pepper

Melt butter in a saucepan. Add onion, carrot, celery, garlic, mushrooms and peppercorns. Cook over medium heat for 5 minutes. Add flour and simmer until flour turns golden brown. Gradually stir in the White Stock, whipping continuously until sauce is smooth. Bring to a boil and simmer for 20 minutes. Remove from heat. In a bowl, beat together cream, egg yolks, and wine; stir mixture into hot sauce. Cook over moderately high heat, stirring constantly until sauce is reduced to a velvety texture. Strain sauce through a fine sieve and season to taste with salt and pepper. Yields 5 cups.

VARIATIONS

SAUCE SUPREME

Follow the directions for Sauce Velouté, but instead of White Stock, use Chicken Broth (see index).

SAUCE IVOIRE

Mix 1 cup Sauce Supreme with 2 tablespoons Meat Glaze (see index).

SAUCE ALBUFERA

Mix 1 cup Sauce Supreme with ½ cup veal gravy and finish with 2 tablespoons pimiento butter (half pimiento and half butter, mashed and rubbed through a sieve).

An outstanding sauce for beef, this is one of the great French sauces.

SAUCE BOURGUIGNONNE
(MUSHROOM SAUCE)

½ cup sliced mushrooms

4 tablespoons butter

½ cup dry red wine

1 cup Brown Sauce (see index)

In a saucepan sauté mushrooms in 2 tablespoons of the butter until golden brown. Remove mushrooms and set aside. Add wine to saucepan, and reduce wine to half its volume over medium heat. Add Brown Sauce. Bring mixture to a boil. Add mushrooms and the remaining 2 tablespoons butter. Spoon on prepared dish just before serving. Yields 2 cups.

A perfect hollandaise is always worth the effort it takes to make it. Its delicate flavor is well suited to vegetables such as broccoli and cauliflower. This sauce is served warm, not hot. It should not be allowed to cook after it has been prepared.

SAUCE HOLLANDAISE

¼ cup white wine vinegar

1 teaspoon crushed white peppercorns

4 egg yolks, slightly beaten

1 tablespoon boiling water

1½ cups melted butter

juice of one lemon

¼ teaspoon salt

In a small saucepan, reduce vinegar with pepper to half its volume over medium heat. Let cool. In a bowl, combine egg yolks with boiling water and add to vinegar. Put mixture in the top of a small double boiler. Place over hot (not boiling) water. (Water below should not touch bottom of pan). Beat mixture with a wire whip until smooth and fluffy. Add melted butter, little by little, whipping continuously. When all butter is added, add lemon juice and salt. Should sauce begin to curdle, remove from heat and beat in 1 tablespoon of boiling water. This sauce should be creamy and velvety when completed.

According to many experts, this sauce is the best in French classical cookery. It is a sauce for meats.

SAUCE BEARNAISE

1/3 cup white wine vinegar

½ cup dry white wine

1 tablespoon peeled and chopped shallots

1 tablespoon dried tarragon leaves

1 tablespoon dried chervil leaves

1 sprig fresh thyme

5 crushed peppercorns

1 tablespoon Meat Glaze (see index)

4 egg yolks, slightly beaten

1 tablespoon water

1 cup melted butter

juice of one lemon

¼ teaspoon each salt, pepper and cayenne

In a small saucepan, combine vinegar, wine, shallots, 1½ teaspoons of the tarragon, 1½ teaspoons of the chervil, the thyme, peppercorns, and meat glaze. Reduce mixture to one-third its volume over medium heat. Cool. In a bowl, combine egg yolks with boiling water and add to vinegar. Put mixture in the top of a small double boiler, and place over hot (not boiling) water. (Water below should not touch bottom of pan.) Beat mixture with wire whip until smooth and fluffy. Add melted butter, little by little, whipping continuously. When all butter is added, add lemon juice, salt, pepper, and cayenne. Add the remaining 1½ teaspoons tarragon and 1½ teaspoons chervil. Yields slightly over 2 cups.

SAUCE AMERICAINE
(AMERICAN SAUCE OR LOBSTER SAUCE)

2 1¾-pound lobsters, uncooked

½ cup oil

¼ teaspoon each, salt and pepper

½ cup shallots, sliced

2 garlic cloves, crushed

½ cup onions, sliced

½ cup carrots, sliced

½ cup celery, sliced

2 sprigs parsley

2 thyme leaves

2 basil leaves

1 bay leaf

½ cup cognac

½ cup white wine

2 cups tomatoes, chopped

½ cup tomato purée

2 cups White Wine and Fish Sauce (see index)

½ cup Meat Glaze

3 tablespoons butter

¼ teaspoon cayenne pepper

Sever the spinal cord of the lobster by inserting a sharp knife at the base of the tail. Cut lobster tail into four pieces and remove the meat. Split the front part and discard the sand bag. Reserve the coral and lobster liquid. Crack the claws and remove the meat.

Heat oil in a saucepan and add the lobster pieces. Season with salt and pepper and let cook until very red. Skim off the excess oil. Add the shallots, garlic, onions, carrots, celery, parsley, thyme, basil and bay leaves and cook for 10 minutes. Add cognac, ignite, and then add the wine. Let cook for 5 more minutes. Add tomato purée, White Wine and Fish Sauce, and Meat Glaze. Bring to a boil and let simmer for 30 minutes. Pour into a colander and remove the lobster meat. Strain mixture through a fine sieve and put back into saucepan. Fold in the coral, mixed with the liquid and butter, mashed and rubbed through a sieve. Adjust seasoning with salt and pepper and add cayenne pepper. Dice lobster meat and add to sauce.

Homemade mayonnaise is amazingly simple to make if you follow the directions. The one trick in making it is to be sure to have all ingredients at room temperature when you begin.

MAYONNAISE

4 egg yolks (at room temperature)

1 teaspoon dry mustard

1 teaspoon salt

¼ teaspoon pepper

1 tablespoon vinegar

2 cups vegetable oil

1 tablespoon boiling water

juice of one lemon

Put egg yolks in small bowl of electric mixer. Add mustard and salt and pepper. Beat at medium speed until well blended. Add vinegar. Continuing to beat, *very* slowly, add oil (literally drop-by-drop, until the sauce begins to thicken). When all the oil has been added, stir in boiling water and lemon juice. Keep sauce in a cold place and use as needed. Yields 2½ cups.

SAUCE NEIGE

Blend together one third sour cream and two thirds mayonnaise.

This sauce is delicious on fried fish and cold seafood.

SAUCE REMOULADE

1 cup mayonnaise (see index)

½ teaspoon dry mustard

1 teaspoon chopped anchovies

1 tablespoon chopped dill pickle

1 tablespoon chopped, fresh parsley

¼ cup sour cream

¼ teaspoon each, salt and pepper

juice of ½ lemon

In a bowl, combine all ingredients and blend well. Yields 1½ cups.

COLD SAUCES SERVED AT THE GREENBRIER

CURRIED MAYONNAISE

Cook 1 tablespoon of curry powder with ½ cup tarragon vinegar and 1 teaspoon sugar. When reduced to a paste, add 1 cup of mayonnaise, ½ cup sour cream, and season to taste.

SAUCE NIÇOISE

Add 2 finely chopped pimientos, ¼ cup tomato purée, and a few tarragon leaves to 2 cups mayonnaise. Pass through a coarse sieve, and add ½ cup sour cream.

GLAÇAGE

Mix equal parts of Sauce Hollandaise and Sauce Velouté or Sauce Béchamel.

SAUCE PARISIENNE

Soften ½ cup cream cheese; season with salt and paprika; add to 2 cups mayonnaise, and garnish with chopped chervil or chives. Finish with 1 cup sour cream.

SAUCE CHANTILLY

Mix 2 cups very thick mayonnaise with 2 cups well-whipped cream and finish with juice of 1 lemon. Season with salt and ground white pepper.

SAUCE ANDALOUSE

Add 1 cup tomato paste to 4 cups mayonnaise and 1 cup sour cream. Garnish with diced sweet peppers and chives.

SAUCE ITALIENNE

Force 1 cup calves brains, cleaned, poached, and cooled, through a fine sieve; add 2 cups mayonnaise. Finish with juice of 1 lemon. Garnish with chopped parsley.

SAUCE VENITIENNE

(Also called Sauce Verte) To 1 cup mayonnaise, add 2 tablespoons of herbs (watercress, parsley, chervil, tarragon) that have been blanched and pounded. Then strain. Finish with juice of 1 lemon. Season with salt and pepper.

SAUCE AIOLI

In a small mortar (or electric blender), pound finely 5 cloves of garlic. Add 2 raw egg yolks and a pinch of salt. Slowly add 2 cups of olive oil, added drop by drop. From time to time, add a few drops lemon juice and thin with water to desired consistency.

SAUCE REMICK

To 1 cup mayonnaise, add 1 cup chili sauce, 1 tablespoon Worcestershire sauce, ½ teaspoon paprika, 1 teaspoon dry mustard, and pinch of celery salt.

EGGS

The egg is probably the most versatile food we have. An egg can be boiled, poached, shirred, fried, coddled, baked, or scrambled. Eggs can be combined with any number of cheeses and herbs to produce a variety of omelettes. An egg can lend its consistency to a soufflé. Hard-cooked eggs can be added to salads and sauces or can simply be served with caviar. Eggs can be deviled or pickled. Their uses are limitless.

Egg whites are considered the most delicate of thickeners and binders and are one of the most important ingredients in meringue and other fluffy delights. Egg yolks are an important ingredient in the preparation of many basic sauces. Eggs add flavor to many dishes, and they can be mixed with a variety of sauces to become entrées. In the kitchens at The Greenbrier, the egg is supreme. Use it in good health!

SHIRRED EGGS

Butter a preheated shallow baking dish. Break eggs (allow 2 eggs per serving) into dish. Salt lightly over whites but not yolks (to keep from discoloring them). Set baking dish in preheated broiler about 4 inches from heat. When yolks are glossy and whites are set, remove dish from broiler. Serve in baking dish. For fried eggs, baste several times with a little boiling water while broiling, and when cooked, cut eggs out in rounds with a 2½ inch cookie cutter.

CODDLED EGGS

Plunge a raw egg (at room temperature) into a pan of boiling water and remove pan from heat. Cover and let stand for 4 minutes for soft and 6 minutes for firmer eggs.

AU GRATIN EGGS

Poached eggs, sliced hard-cooked eggs, or an omelette can be used for Au Gratin Eggs simply by covering prepared eggs with Sauce Mornay (see index) and sprinkling with grated cheese. Set in preheated 400°F. oven for a few minutes to brown cheese lightly.

SCALLOPED EGGS

Cover sliced, hard-cooked eggs with equal parts of Newburg Sauce, cream, and sherry, all of which have been heated. Or, top with a few sliced onions, sautéed in a little butter, and cover with cream.

OEUFS BROUILLES A LA FRANÇAISE
(FRENCH-STYLE SCRAMBLED EGGS)

Half fill bottom of a double boiler with hot water, and place over low heat. Melt 2 tablespoons butter in top of double boiler and add 2 slightly beaten eggs. Place over simmering water, and stir with a wire whip until eggs begin to cook. Stir in 1 tablespoon butter and 2 tablespoons heavy cream. Add 4 tablespoons Bèchamel Sauce (see index); mix well and serve when eggs are still slightly moist. Serves one.

FRENCH OMELETTE

The difficulty in preparing an omelette is more imagined than real. Success is assured, if the following points are observed.

1.   The pan is most important. Many cooks keep a pan that is used only for omelettes. It should have rounded sides, and the surface should be completely smooth and seasoned. An 8-to-10-inch size is best for a 4-egg omelette that serves two. (When serving more than two, it is best to make several omelettes. Wipe the pan with a paper towel before starting each one.) If a pan that is used for other cooking must be used, scrub it with a steel wool pad until it is smooth. Season it by putting a little vegetable oil in the bottom and setting it over moderate heat for 15 to 20 minutes. Pour off oil and wipe dry with paper towels.

2.   The eggs should be at room temperature and utensils should be within easy reach before you start.

3.   Beat the eggs with a fork until well blended, but not frothy, just before pre-heating omelette pan.

The following will make an omelette to serve two.

In a bowl, put 4 eggs, ¼ teaspoon salt, and a few grains pepper. Beat with a fork until eggs are blended but not frothy. Heat 1½ tablespoons butter in an 8-to-10-inch skillet over high heat. As butter melts tilt pan to coat bottom and sides. When butter stops foaming and before it starts to turn color, pour in eggs. After a few seconds, eggs will partially set on the bottom. Then with the flat side of the fork, stir eggs in a circular motion and at the same time shake the pan back and forth over the heat; omelette should move freely. Cook only until top is like custard. Tilt handle of pan up and, with the fork, loosen edge nearest handle rolling one-third of the omelette to the center. Slip it to the far edge of the pan, roll again so seam is underneath. Slide omelette onto a warm serving plate.

AMERICAN-STYLE SCRAMBLED EGGS

Melt 1 tablespoon butter in small skillet, and break 2 unbeaten eggs into it. Mix eggs with a fork while cooking over low heat. Gather into the middle the parts of the eggs that have begun to cook, and remove from heat while still slightly moist; season with salt and pepper, and serve immediately. You will note that American-Style Scrambled Eggs will be streaked with yolk and white and will be lumpy, as opposed to the smooth uniformly colored French style.

POACHED EGGS

Carefully break eggs into a shallow skillet that is three-fourths full of simmering water (add a dash of salt and ½ teaspoon vinegar for each cup of water). Let eggs cook 3 to 5 minutes, depending on firmness desired. Remove eggs with a slotted spoon and serve immediately, or if they are to be used later, place in cold water. When ready to use, reheat in hot water.

OEUFS FRITS
(FRIED EGGS FRENCH STYLE)

Heat vegetable oil in a small frying pan over moderately high heat, using enough oil for the egg to float. Carefully break egg into a cup and season with salt. Slip egg into heated oil and, with two wooden spoons, gather the white around the yolk until it is sealed by the hot oil. Wait two minutes; remove egg, and drain on paper towel. Garnish with fresh parsley sprigs quickly fried in the same oil.

FRITTATA OMELETTE

Break 4 eggs into a bowl; beat them well with a wire whip. Melt about 1 tablespoon butter in a medium-sized skillet over low heat. Add eggs. Do not disturb until mixture begins to set on top side; turn like a pancake with a spatula and cook on second side until light golden brown. Serve on hot plate. Serves two.

SOFT-COOKED EGG

Plunge egg (at room temperature) into pan of simmering water. Cook for 3 minutes. Remove and cool egg very briefly in cold water to prevent further cooking.

HARD-COOKED EGG

Plunge egg (at room temperature) into a pan of simmering water for 10 minutes. Remove egg and place into cold water. Peel under cold running water. Keep it in cold water until used for the recipe chosen.

OEUFS EN COCOTTE
(EGGS IN BAKING DISH)

Warm a small individual baking dish. Generously butter inside. Break 2 eggs into the dish and set dish in a larger pan of hot water. Bake in preheated oven at 375°F. for 8 minutes or until cooked to firmness desired. Serves one.

OEUFS EN MOULES
(EGGS IN MOLD)

Generously coat the inside of a small soufflé mold or baking dish with butter and sprinkle with parsley (or you may use finely chopped ham). Break 4 eggs into the lined mold, and set dish in a large pan of hot water. Bake in preheated 375°F. oven for 12 minutes. Serve on croutons. Serves two.

Morels are the most flavorful of mushrooms and add great zest to an omelette. If you cannot find them you may substitute fresh mushrooms. This is a delicious luncheon omelette.

OMELETTE AUX MORILLES GRATINE GENEVOISE
(OMELETTE WITH MORELS)

½ cup dried morels

1 shallot, peeled and chopped

2 tablespoons butter

1 teaspoon lemon juice

¼ teaspoon salt

¼ teaspoon pepper

½ cup heavy cream

1 teaspoon Meat Glaze (see index)

French Omelette made with 6 eggs (see index)

½ cup Sauce Glaçage (see index)

Soak morels in lukewarm water. When soft, carefully cut off ends of the morels. Wash thoroughly to remove sand. Sauté shallot in butter over medium heat until golden brown. Add morels, lemon juice, salt and pepper, and sauté lightly; add heavy cream and Meat Glaze, and simmer for 5 minutes. Make French Omelette (see index) using the morel mixture as a filling (add just before folding omelette over). Turn omelette out onto a heat-proof platter and top with Sauce Glaçage. Brown lightly in preheated broiler. Serves two.

The favorite omelette at The Greenbrier.

FRITTATA OMELETTE VIRGINIA
(FLAT VIRGINIA OMELETTE)

4 teaspoons butter

4 tablespoons diced, cooked Virginia ham

6 eggs, slightly beaten

4 tablespoons melted cheddar cheese

Heat a 6-inch skillet over moderate heat and melt the butter. Add the ham and sauté for 30 seconds. Add eggs; mix well, and spread mixture evenly over the bottom of the skillet. Cook over low heat, being careful not to disturb mixture until top has a uniformly soft, golden color. Turn omelette onto a plate and top with melted cheese. Serves two to three.

A delightful breakfast, brunch or luncheon creation that appears often on the menu at The Greenbrier.

OEUFS BENEDICT
(EGGS BENEDICT)

4 English muffins, split

*8 thin slices cooked
Virginia ham or Canadian bacon*

8 poached eggs

½ cup warm Hollandaise Sauce (see index)

8 ripe olives, pitted and cut in half

Place muffins, split side up, on a broiler tray. Toast in a preheated broiler about 3 inches from heat. Remove and keep warm. Arrange ham or bacon slices on the same broiler tray and heat gently in broiler. Meanwhile, poach eggs. Arrange 2 muffin halves, toasted side up on each serving plate. Put a slice of ham or bacon on each half. Put a poached egg on ham and spoon Hollandaise Sauce over eggs. Garnish with ripe olives. Serves four.

GRAINS AND PASTAS

Grains and pastas are versatile foods. They can be combined with numerous spices and seasonings for distinctive, flavorful treats. They supplement vegetables and meats in main dishes, and they are quite delicious when left to stand on their own merits— cooked to perfection, lightly covered with butter or cream, and perhaps tossed gently with an herb or cheese.

Pastas and grains are available in too many forms to list separately here. A large selection can be found in most grocery stores, and you should make an effort to experiment as much as possible.

The collection of recipes that follows is small but varied. I have included a pasta recipe for ravioli; it can also be used to make other pastas. There is a special recipe for wild rice, followed by several interesting variations.

Ravioli was originally developed as a means of using left-overs. Today, it belies any such humble beginning.

RAVIOLI
Ravioli Filling

½ cup chopped, cooked lean beef

2 cups chopped washed spinach

½ cup raw ground veal

¼ cup chopped shallots,
sautéed in 1 tablespoon butter until soft

¼ cup (2 ounces) cream cheese

¼ cup grated Parmesan cheese

2 whole eggs

1 teaspoon salt

1 teaspoon allspice

½ teaspoon peeled, minced garlic

Combine all ingredients. Put mixture through a food grinder with a coarse blade. Cover and store in refrigerator until needed.

Tomato Sauce

4 tablespoons butter

6 medium tomatoes, peeled and cubed

1 teaspoon minced, peeled garlic

½ teaspoon salt

¼ teaspoon pepper

2 tablespoons tomato purée

2 cups Chicken Broth (see index)

2 teaspoons flour

2 tablespoons cold water

1 teaspoon sugar

1 cup grated Parmesan cheese (reserve for garnish)

Heat butter in a saucepan. Add tomatoes, garlic, salt and pepper. Cook over high heat 5 minutes. Stir in tomato purée and Chicken Broth. Combine flour, water, and sugar, and stir into tomato mixture. Bring to a boil and simmer uncovered 30 minutes. Remove from heat. Reheat just before using. Garnish with Parmesan cheese.

Ravioli Dough

1 egg, slightly beaten

2 tablespoons warm water

2 tablespoons vegetable oil

1½ cups all-purpose flour

½ teaspoon salt

Lightly mix egg with warm water and oil. Put flour in a bowl, add salt, egg mixed with water and oil. Knead dough on a well-floured pastry board with floured hands until smooth and elastic, about 10 minutes. Cover and let stand for one hour. When dough is ready, roll it paper-thin on well-floured pastry board, and cut into 3-inch squares.

To Assemble: Drop scant teaspoonsful of the filling on each square. Wet edges with water (using pastry brush). Lay a second square over the filled one, and seal edges together with fingers or a fork. Cook for 15 minutes in a large kettle of boiling water. Remove with slotted spoon. Arrange ravioli on platter, and cover with the hot Tomato Sauce. Sprinkle with the 1 cup grated Parmesan cheese. Brown lightly under broiler. Serves eight.

The Romans served an early version of gnocchi, a type of dumpling, which was one of the first creations of professional cooks.

GNOCCHI
(DUMPLINGS)

2 cups all-purpose flour

3 eggs, slightly beaten

1/3 cup water

½ teaspoon salt

¼ teaspoon pepper

¼ teaspoon nutmeg

3 quarts boiling water to which ½ teaspoon salt has been added

3 tablespoons butter

1/3 cup dry bread crumbs, sautéed in 1 tablespoon butter

In a bowl, combine flour, eggs, 1/3 cup water, ½ teaspoon salt, pepper and nutmeg. Beat with a wooden spoon until smooth. Pinch off small pieces of the dough and roll into small balls with the hands. Drop balls into boiling salted water in a large saucepan. When the gnocchi come to the surface, they are cooked. Remove with a slotted spoon and drain on paper towels. Heat butter in a large skillet until golden brown. Add gnocchi and sauté them until very hot. Place them in a serving dish and top with browned bread crumbs. Grated cheese or sour cream may be served with the dumplings, if desired. Serves eight.

GNOCCHI A LA ROMAINE
(SEMOLINA OR FARINA WITH CHEESE)

1 quart milk

2 tablespoons butter

¼ teaspoon each, salt and nutmeg

1 cup semolina or farina

½ cup grated Parmesan cheese

2 eggs, slightly beaten

2 tablespoons melted butter

Bring milk to a rolling boil in a large saucepan. Add butter, salt, and nutmeg. Slowly add semolina or farina, stirring constantly until thickened and smooth. Cook over low heat for 15 minutes or until mixture pulls away from sides of pan. Remove from heat and add ¼ cup Parmesan cheese and eggs. Mix well and let cool for 10 minutes. Spread mixture one-half inch thick in a shallow buttered pan. Place in refrigerator to chill. When cooled, cut into half moons with a cookie cutter and arrange in a shallow oven-proof dish. Top with remaining cheese and butter. Preheat oven to 350°F. (moderate). Bake gnocchi 20 minutes or until browned. They should be fluffy. Serves four.

This is a simple dish to prepare, and a tasty, delicate side dish for numerous entrées.

NOUILLES A L'ALFREDO
(NOODLES WITH CREAM AND CHEESE)

½ pound egg noodles

2 egg yolks

1/3 cup heavy cream

1/3 cup soft butter

1/3 cup grated Parmesan cheese

¼ teaspoon each, salt, pepper, and nutmeg

Cook the noodles in boiling salted water according to package directions. Drain and put them into a heated bowl. In a bowl whip egg yolks until foamy, add the cream and gradually the butter. Now mix in the cheese, and season with salt, pepper and nutmeg. Pour egg mixture onto very hot noodles and mix thoroughly. Serve immediately on very hot plates. Serves six.

This is an elegant variation of the usual spaghetti with meat sauce. Clams are generally inexpensive and widely available in fish markets throughout the United States. The fines herbes referred to in the recipe is a mixture of herbs, usually including equal parts of parsley, tarragon, chives, and chervil. In this case, you might want to include oregano or basil to complement the tomatoes.

SPAGHETTI ALLE VONGOLE
(SPAGHETTI WITH CLAMS)

2 dozen clams, scrubbed

1/3 cup peeled, chopped shallots

3 garlic cloves, peeled, crushed, and chopped

½ cup dry white wine

3 tablespoons butter

1 cup peeled, diced tomatoes

1 tablespoon fines herbes

½ pound spaghetti

1/3 cup grated Parmesan cheese

Discard any clams that are not tightly closed. Scrub well under cold, running water. Rinse thoroughly. Place clams in a 4-quart saucepan; add shallots, garlic, and wine. Cover tightly and cook until clam shells open, about 3 minutes. Remove clams and shells from saucepan and reserve. Reduce remaining liquid to half its volume, then strain. Melt butter in a saucepan. Remove clams from shells and add to butter. Sauté for one minute. Add tomatoes, fines herbes, and reduced liquid and cook 2 minutes longer. Do not over-cook. Cook spaghetti in boiling salted water according to package directions. Drain and place in serving dish. Pour hot sauce over spaghetti and serve with grated Parmesan cheese. Serves six.

RIZ PILAF OU PILAW
(RICE PILAF)

1½ tablespoons butter

2 tablespoons peeled, chopped onion

1 cup long-grained rice

2½ cups Chicken Broth (see index)

½ teaspoon salt

¼ teaspoon pepper

Heat butter in a medium-sized skillet, and cook onions slowly for one minute. Add rice and cook until it turns a yellowish color. Add Chicken Broth and bring to a boil. Cover and let simmer for 20 minutes, until rice is tender and liquid is absorbed. Season with salt and pepper. Serves six.

TURKISH RICE

Follow the same procedure as for Rice Pilaf but replace half of the Chicken Broth with tomato juice, and add 1 pinch saffron to the rice while it is cooking.

RISOTTO A LA PIEMONTAISE
(RICE COOKED IN CHEESE AND CHICKEN BROTH)

½ cup butter

2 tablespoons peeled, chopped onion

½ cup sliced mushrooms

1 cup long-grained rice

*2½ cups Chicken Broth (see index)
heated to boiling*

½ cup grated Parmesan cheese

½ teaspoon salt

¼ teaspoon pepper

Heat ¼ cup of the butter in a saucepan and sauté onion until golden. Add mushrooms and sauté 2 minutes. Add rice and cook for 2 minutes. Add boiling broth and simmer covered for 15 minutes, until rice is tender and liquid is absorbed. Remove from heat and add remaining ¼ cup butter and cheese. Mix well. Add salt, pepper and mushrooms, and serve. Serves six.

RISOTTO A LA MILANAISE
(Saffron Rice)

Follow the same procedure as for Rice cooked in Cheese and Chicken Broth, but add 1 pinch saffron to the rice before adding broth and omit mushrooms.

RIZ SAUVAGE
(WILD RICE)

1 cup wild rice

2½ cups water

½ teaspoon salt plus ¼ teaspoon salt

2 tablespoons butter

¼ teaspoon pepper

Wash rice thoroughly. Bring water and ½ teaspoon of the salt to a boil in a saucepan; add rice. Cover and cook slowly for about 45 minutes, until rice is tender. Drain and rinse with hot water. Add butter, ¼ teaspoon of the salt, and pepper. Serve hot. Serves four.

VARIATIONS

BUTTERED WILD RICE

Sauté 1 cup of cooked, drained rice in 2 tablespoons butter until thoroughly heated.

BUTTERED WILD RICE WITH CURRY

Season 2 cups of cooked wild rice with 2 teaspoons curry powder, and garnish with ½ cup diced pineapple, 1 sliced banana, ½ of a peeled, chopped apple and red cherries.

WILD RICE WITH RED CURRANT JELLY

Butter 2 cups cooked wild rice, and mix with 2 tablespoons red currant jelly until rice is well coated.

WILD RICE FOR STUFFING

Mix 1 cup cooked wild rice with ¼ cup goose liver paste, ¼ cup sautéed chopped chicken livers flavored with 3 tablespoons brandy. This stuffing is used for poultry, quail, pheasant, guinea hen, and pigeon.

SEAFOOD

The waters of the world contain an enormous variety of seafood. Not everyone is fortunate enough to live in an area near water where fresh fish is available, but modern transportation systems and the quick-freezing techniques used today permit most people to obtain an adequate supply of fresh fish or frozen fish that has a quality approaching that of freshly caught fish. Because of the freezing techniques, also, it is possible to obtain not only native American seafoods, such as lobster, oysters, salmon, pompano, red snapper, and shrimp, but a variety of seafoods from all over the world.

It is important to know how to select fresh seafood. The freshness of fish can be determined in several ways. Select fish with firm flesh, which should be elastic and readily spring back when touched; a clean, fresh smell; bright eyes and scales; and bright reddish-pink gills. Since fish deteriorate quickly, these characteristics are extremely important. Lobsters should generally be purchased alive and cooked shortly after purchasing.

The recipes that follow are long-standing favorites at The Greenbrier.

A delicate, fluffy fish mousse, covered with a rich sauce, is a spectacular way to start a meal. This one, made with fillet of sole, is outstanding.

MOUSSE DE SOLES A L'AMIRAL
(MOUSSE OF SOLE ADMIRAL)

1½ pounds fillet of sole

1 cup Fish Stock (see index)

4 egg whites, unbeaten

1 cup heavy cream

¼ teaspoon salt

¼ teaspoon pepper

¼ teaspoon cayenne

1 cup American Sauce (see index)

Preheat oven to 350°F. Cut fillets into bite-sized pieces, and purée in an electric blender, a small amount at a time. Put puréed mixture in a bowl and set bowl on ice cubes in a larger bowl. Let stand until well chilled. Add fish stock gradually, then add the egg whites and cream, and mix to a smooth consistency. Add salt, pepper, and cayenne. Pour into a 3-quart mold, filling it only ¾ full. Place the mold in a pan half-filled with hot water and bake at 350°F. for 15 minutes. Heat American Sauce in a separate pan, but do not boil. When mousse is done, unmold onto a hot platter. Ladle sauce over mousse. Serve with a rice pilaf. Serves six.

PAUPIETTES DE SOLES GREENBRIER
(ROLLED SOLE GREENBRIER)

1/3 cup peeled, chopped shallots

½ cup butter

1 cup chopped fresh mushrooms

¼ cup chopped fresh parsley

1/3 cup fresh breadcrumbs

2 egg yolks, slightly beaten

½ teaspoon each, salt and pepper

8 fillets of sole, 4 ounces each

½ cup dry vermouth

½ cup heavy cream

½ cup grated Parmesan cheese

3 tablespoons butter

Preheat oven to 375°F. Sauté shallots in the ½ cup butter over low heat in a small saucepan until tender. Add mushrooms and cook 1 minute. Add parsley, breadcrumbs, and egg yolks. Mix quickly and remove from heat. Add salt and pepper. Spread fillets evenly with mushroom mixture. Roll up each fillet. Place rolls in a shallow baking dish. Mix vermouth and cream, and pour over rolls. Sprinkle with grated cheese and dot top with the 3 tablespoons butter. Bake in 375°F. for 20 minutes. Serves eight.

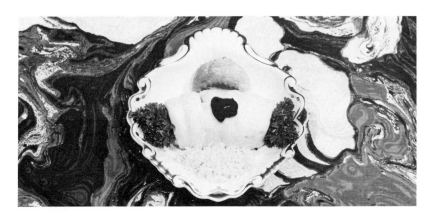

Pompano, widely available in Florida, is considered by many to be the finest saltwater fish available in the United States.

FILET DE POMPANO AUX AMANDES
(FILLET OF POMPANO WITH ALMONDS)

4 fillets of pompano, 8 ounces each

1 cup milk

¼ teaspoon salt

¼ teaspoon pepper

1/3 cup all-purpose flour

½ cup butter

1 lemon, cut in half

3 tablespoons butter

½ cup sliced, blanched almonds

Marinate fillets in milk and salt and pepper for 10 minutes. Remove fillets and pat dry with paper towel. Dust both sides of fillets lightly with flour. Melt the ½ cup butter in a heavy skillet and place fish in it. Brown 4 minutes on each side. Remove fish to a heated serving platter and squeeze lemon juice on them. Melt the remaining 3 tablespoons butter in a skillet, add almonds and sauté until brown. Sprinkle browned almonds over fish and serve immediately. Serves four.

Red snapper is another delightful fish from our shores; meaty and high in flavor, it can be prepared in almost any fashion.

FILET DE ROUGET DE MER PROVENÇALE
(FILLET OF RED SNAPPER PROVENÇALE)

6 fillets of red snapper, 8 ounces each

½ teaspoon salt

¼ teaspoon pepper

1/3 cup all-purpose flour

½ cup vegetable oil

1 lemon, cut in half

3 tablespoons butter

1/3 cup peeled, finely chopped shallots

2 garlic cloves, peeled, crushed, and chopped

2 cups peeled, chopped tomatoes

1 tablespoon chopped, fresh parsley

Wash fish and wipe dry. Season with salt and pepper, and roll fillets lightly in flour. Heat oil in heavy skillet. Add fillets and sauté until golden brown; turn and brown other side. Place fillets on heated platter, and squeeze lemon juice on them. Melt butter in skillet; add shallots and garlic, and sauté until golden brown. Add tomatoes and reduce mixture over high heat to a slightly thickened consistency. Pour sauce over fish, and sprinkle with chopped parsley. Serves six.

Frog legs are a great specialty, but they are difficult to find fresh, so you may have to depend on your frozen food section.

CUISSES DE GRENOUILLES PROVENÇALE
(FROG LEGS PROVENÇALE)

24 frog legs

½ teaspoon salt

¼ teaspoon pepper

½ cup vegetable oil

1/3 cup chopped shallots

1 garlic clove, peeled, crushed, and chopped

½ cup peeled, chopped fresh tomatoes

juice of one lemon

2 tablespoons chopped fresh parsley

2 tablespoons soft butter

Clean frog legs and pat dry with paper towel; sprinkle with salt and pepper. Heat oil in a large skillet, and add frog legs. Sauté until golden brown on both sides. When a fork enters meat easily, drain off oil. Add shallots and garlic. Sauté for 2 minutes. Add the tomatoes; cover and let simmer for 2 more minutes. Remove to a heated platter, sprinkle with lemon juice, and garnish with chopped parsley. Top with the butter, which has been heated until golden brown. Serve at once. Serves four.

This is a simple dish and, at the same time, extremely tasty.

FILET DE BAR DORIA
(FILLET OF STRIPED BASS DORIA)

4 fillets of striped bass, 6 ounces each

½ cup milk

1 tablespoon flour

½ teaspoon salt

¼ teaspoon pepper

½ cup butter

1 garlic clove, peeled and halved

1 cup diced cucumbers

1 lemon, cut in half

½ teaspoon chopped fresh parsley

Dip fillets into the milk and then dust lightly with flour and sprinkle with salt and pepper. Melt butter with garlic in a heavy skillet. Add fillets and sauté until golden brown. Turn and brown other side. Remove fillets to a warm serving plate. Remove garlic halves from butter remaining in skillet. Add cucumbers and sauté for 2 minutes. Remove cucumbers from skillet and place them on top of fillets. Squeeze lemon juice over fillets, and top with chopped parsley. Serves four.

LAITANCE D'ALOSE AUX AMANDES
(SHAD ROE WITH ALMONDS)

4 shad roe, 10 ounces each

¼ teaspoon each, salt and pepper

1 tablespoon flour

½ cup butter

juice of 2 lemons

3 tablespoons butter

½ cup blanched, slivered almonds

Wash roe and sprinkle with salt, pepper, and flour. Melt ½ cup butter in a skillet over low heat, and sauté roe until golden brown (about 8 minutes). Place roe on heated platter and drizzle with lemon juice. Melt 3 tablespoons butter in skillet; add almonds and sauté them until golden brown. Top roe with the almonds. Serves four.

TORTUE TERRAPENE BALTIMORE
(TERRAPIN BALTIMORE)

4 cups terrapin meat, fresh or frozen

½ cup butter

1 cup dry sherry

1 cup Meat Glaze (see index)

4 tablespoons brandy

dash cayenne

Melt ¼ cup of the butter in a saucepan. Add terrapin and cook for 15 minutes over low heat. Add wine and Meat Glaze, and simmer for 3 minutes. Add remaining ¼ cup butter, brandy, and cayenne. Heat gently and serve in a chafing dish. Serves four.

CRABES MOUX A LA MEUNIERE
(SOFT SHELL CRABS MEUNIERE)

12 soft shell crabs, cleaned

½ cup light cream

½ cup all-purpose flour

½ cup vegetable oil

3 tablespoons butter

juice of 1 lemon

½ cup chopped fresh parsley

Wash crabs well. Dip each one in cream, and roll in flour to coat both sides lightly. Heat oil in large skillet, and sauté crabs until brown on both sides (about 5 minutes on each side). Put on heated platter. Drain oil from skillet. Add butter and heat until it is melted. Pour butter over crabs; squeeze lemon juice over them, and sprinkle with parsley. Serves four.

This traditional Creole dish hails from New Orleans, where it has been a favorite for years.

CREVETTES JAMBALAYA
(SHRIMP JAMBALAYA)

2 medium-sized green peppers, washed and seeded

½ cup vegetable oil

1 onion, peeled and sliced

2 garlic cloves, peeled and chopped

½ pound mushrooms, sliced

4 tomatoes, peeled and chopped

½ cup tomato purée

1 cup dry white wine

1 cup Fish Stock (see index)

¼ cup butter

1 cup cubed, boiled ham

2½ pounds raw shrimp, shelled and deveined

2 cups fresh okra, cut into ½-inch lengths

salt and pepper to taste

Cut peppers into 1½ inch strips, and sauté in heated oil in a large saucepan. Add onions, garlic, and mushrooms. Cook over medium heat until liquid has reduced to half its volume. Add tomatoes, purée, wine, and Fish Stock, and bring to a boil. Simmer uncovered for 10 minutes; set aside. In another saucepan, melt butter; add ham, shrimp, and okra. Cook for 5 minutes over moderate heat. Add vegetable mixture to shrimp and cook 5 minutes longer. Season to taste with salt and pepper. Serves six.

Lobster takes on an interesting and intriguing taste when curry is added. The coconut milk this recipe calls for is not readily available. A substitute can be made by soaking packaged shredded coconut in hot milk.

CURRIE DE LANGOUSTE
(CURRIED ROCK LOBSTER)

4 medium size frozen lobster tails, thawed

¼ cup vegetable oil

½ cup peeled and chopped onions

3 garlic cloves, peeled,crushed, and chopped

¼ teaspoon each salt and pepper

2 tablespoons curry powder

2 tablespoons flour

1 cup Fish Stock (see index)

1 cup dry white wine

2 tablespoons tomato purée

½ cup fresh coconut milk

1/3 cup heavy cream

1 cup peeled and diced apples

Boil lobster tails for 5 minutes in water to cover. Remove lobster meat from shells and cut it into ½-inch cubes. Heat oil in a saucepan; add onions and garlic. Cook for 2 minutes. Add lobster meat, salt and pepper, curry, flour, Fish Stock, wine, and tomato purée. Cook over medium heat 15 minutes, stirring constantly. Strain mixture through a coarse sieve to remove lobster from sauce. Reserve lobster. Cook sauce until reduced to one-half its volume. Add coconut milk and cream, and simmer for 5 minutes. Add apples and reserved lobster and simmer for 5 minutes. Serve with Rice Pilaf, if desired. Serves four.

MOULES MARINIERES
(STEWED MUSSELS)

4 quarts mussels

1 teaspoon peeled, chopped shallots

1 teaspoon peeled, chopped onions

1 teaspoon chopped, fresh parsley

1 cup dry white wine

4 tablespoons butter

2 teaspoons flour

salt and pepper to taste

Discard any mussels that are not tightly closed. Scrub well under cold running water. With a sharp knife, trim off the beard around the edges. Rinse thoroughly. Place mussels in a large saucepan with shallots, onions, parsley, and wine. Cover tightly and cook over medium heat until shells open. Pour into collander over a bowl. Put mussels in dish in which they will be served, and keep warm. Pour cooking juice back into saucepan, taking care not to include sediment that may have settled to the bottom of bowl. Reduce juice to one-third its volume over high heat. Blend butter into the flour. Add to saucepan. Stir until smooth. Add salt and pepper to taste. Pour juice over mussels. Serves four.

If you like Lobster Newburg, you will probably enjoy this interesting variation.

PETONCLES A LA NEWBURG
(SCALLOPS NEWBURG)

1 quart scallops

1 cup dry white wine

½ cup butter plus 3 tablespoons

¼ teaspoon each, salt and pepper

¼ teaspoon paprika

1 cup dry sherry

1½ cups heavy cream

4 egg yolks, slightly beaten

¼ teaspoon cayenne

In a saucepan, simmer scallops in white wine for 5 minutes. Drain off wine into another saucepan. Add ½ cup butter, salt, pepper, paprika, sherry, and ¾ cup of the cream to the drained liquid, and cook for 5 minutes over medium heat. Add a little of the hot sauce to the beaten egg yolks and stir egg mixture into the hot sauce. Add remaining ¾ cup cream. When hot, but not boiling, slowly add 3 tablespoons of the butter, and then the scallops. Heat gently 3 minutes. Add cayenne and serve in a chafing dish. Serves four.

BEEF

Beef, undoubtedly the favorite food of most Americans, should be tender, juicy, and flavorful. High quality in meat is indicated by a fine grain, heavy marbling, and a bright to slightly dark red color, depending upon how long the meat has been aged. A high-quality cut of meat requires very little cooking time, and a lower quality requires longer cooking time. In the United States, meat is graded for quality:

U.S. Prime is the best beef you can buy, although it usually is sold to restaurants and is rarely found in grocery stores. Prime meat has a great deal of marbling, making it extremely tender.

Choice is frequently found in markets. It is flavorful and tender.

U.S. Good is fine for use in stews, soups, and some roasts, particularly if most of the fat has been trimmed from it. You should plan to cook this meat a long time, with herbs, spices, and vegetables added for flavor.

U.S. Commercial and *U.S. Utility* are seldom found in markets catering to the general public.

The best cuts for quick cooking in dry heat are fillet, club steak, Porterhouse steak, sirloin, standing rib roast, and rolled rib roast—all tender cuts. (The names of cuts may vary depending upon the part of the country in which you live, but your butcher can always help you find the cut you want regardless of its local name.)

Slower cooking under moist heat is good for cuts such as round steak, rump roast, flank steak, stew meat, short ribs, chuck roast, and brisket. Meats prepared by moist, slow cooking should always be well done, whereas tender cuts may be served rare, medium or well done, depending upon individual tastes.

111

One of the most spectacular and delicious main courses served at The Greenbrier.

FILET DE BOEUF WELLINGTON
(BEEF WELLINGTON)

1 beef tenderloin, about 5 pounds

½ teaspoon salt

½ teaspoon pepper

2 tablespoons butter

½ cup peeled, chopped onion

1 pound fresh mushrooms, chopped

½ pound ground pork

1 cup chicken livers, sliced

½ pound goose liver pâté

2 eggs

1/3 cup brandy

pastry for 9-inch, 2-crust pie

3 sheets pork fat (or 6 strips bacon)

Preheat oven to 450°F. Sprinkle beef lightly with salt and pepper, and place on rack in shallow roasting pan. Roast about 20 minutes per pound for rare. Remove from oven and let cool to room temperature. Melt butter in a skillet and sauté onions until golden brown. Add mushrooms and sauté until browned. Add ground pork and chicken livers and let cook for 3 minutes. Remove from heat and cool mixture to room temperature. Place onion mixture in an electric blender. Add goose liver pâté, one of the eggs and brandy. Blend until smooth. Set this mixture aside for the filling. Prepare pastry dough. Roll dough on a lightly floured board into a rectangle about ⅛-inch thick and large enough to completely enclose tenderloin. Place cooled tenderloin on pastry about 2 inches from one long side. Spread pâté mixture on meat and cover with pork fat or bacon strips. Fold pastry over meat, and seal seam and ends carefully. Place roll in a shallow roasting pan. Lightly beat remaining egg, and brush pastry with it. Preheat oven to 350°F. Bake tenderloin 50 minutes until pastry is golden brown. Serves eight.

ENTRECOTE GRILLEE
(SIRLOIN STEAK)

4 beef sirloin steaks, 1-inch thick

½ teaspoon salt

1 teaspoon freshly ground pepper

2 tablespoons vegetable oil

2 tablespoons butter

Remove the steaks from the refrigerator one hour before broiling. Preheat broiler. Sprinkle both sides with salt and pepper and rub with oil. Place steaks on broiler pan 2 to 3 inches from heat. Broil 3 minutes. Turn gently being sure not to spear meat and broil for 3 minutes more. This will make a very rare steak. For medium, leave steak in broiler for 3 minutes longer. For well done, 5 minutes longer. Heat butter in a skillet and pour over steaks. Serves four.

The marvelous flavor of sirloin can be presented in no better fashion.

CONTRE-FILET DE BOEUF ROTI
(ROAST SIRLOIN OF BEEF)

1 beef sirloin strip, 6 to 8 pounds

½ teaspoon salt

½ teaspoon pepper

¼ cup melted bacon fat

2 onions, peeled and quartered

2 carrots, scraped and sliced

2 celery stalks, sliced

1 garlic clove, peeled and crushed

1 bay leaf

1 teaspoon dried thyme

5 peppercorns

½ cup dry red wine

1 cup Brown Stock (see index)

salt and pepper to taste

Preheat oven to 400°F. Season sirloin strip with salt and pepper, and place in a shallow roasting pan, fat side down with bacon fat. Roast at 400°F. for 25 minutes. Reduce oven temperature to 350°F. Turn meat and roast 25 minutes longer. About 10 minutes before the roast is cooked, add onions, carrots, celery, garlic, bay leaf, thyme, and peppercorns. when meat is done to your preference, take it out of pan and set aside. Return the pan with vegetables to the oven for another 10 minutes. Skim off the fat. Add the wine and Brown Stock, and return pan to oven for 10 minutes longer. Strain; then season to taste with salt and pepper. Slice the beef and pour the sauce over. Serves 6-8.

This dish is braised in its own marinade, creating an exciting taste.

BOEUF A LA CUILLERE OU EN DAUBE
(BRAISED BEEF)

1 sirloin tip roast, 8 pounds

1 cup dry red wine

2 tablespoons vinegar

4 tablespoons peeled, chopped shallots

1 garlic clove, peeled, crushed, and chopped

4 tablespoons chopped, fresh parsley

4 tablespoons chopped, fresh tarragon leaves

1 teaspoon salt

1 teaspoon pepper

2 tablespoons bacon fat

2 cups Sauce au Madère (see index)

6 bacon strips

1 cup all-purpose flour

½ cup water

Put the beef in a large crock or enamel kettle. Add the wine, vinegar, shallots, garlic, parsley, and tarragon. Cover and marinate beef in this mixture for three days. Remove the meat from the marinade. Reserve marinade. Season meat with salt and pepper. Heat bacon fat in a large skillet and brown meat on all sides. Remove and set aside. Drain the fat from the skillet and add the reserved marinade. Bring to a boil and reduce to one-half its volume. Add the Sauce au Madère and simmer for 10 minutes. Preheat oven to 325°F. Grease a large Dutch oven and place the beef in the center of the pot. Place the bacon strips across the top.

Pour sauce over the meat just to cover. Blend flour and water to a smooth paste. Seal the lid on the pot by covering the seam generously with the paste. Bake at 325°F. for 6 hours. Serves six.

Too long looked down upon, few foods are more delicious when well-prepared than hash.

ROAST BEEF HASH AMERICAN

4 cups cold roast beef

1 cup peeled, chopped potatoes

½ cup chopped green peppers

1 cup peeled, chopped onions

½ teaspoon each, salt and pepper

1 cup Beef Stock (see index)

3 tablespoons vegetable oil

6 teaspoons butter

6 poached eggs (see index)

Preheat oven to 275°F. Dice cold beef in small squares and combine with potatoes, peppers, and onions. Add salt and pepper and stir in beef stock. Put mixture in a heat-proof casserole with the vegetable oil; bring to a boil and cover tightly. Bake in 275°F. oven for 3 hours. Melt one teaspoon butter in small frying pan. Add one cupful of hash and sauté on both sides until brown. Turn hash out onto a dinner plate and place one poached egg on top. Repeat with remaining butter and hash until you have six servings.

Ground beef has been abused in too many kitchens; nonetheless, properly prepared, it is a treat that rivals steak.

GROUND BEEF STEAK AMERICAN

2 pounds lean beef round or chuck

½ teaspoon salt

¼ teaspoon pepper

1/3 cup tomato juice

1 tablespoon vegetable oil

4 tablespoons soft butter

Put meat through a food grinder with coarse plate or have butcher grind it. Season with salt and pepper, and mix with tomato juice. Form beef into 4 patties in the shape of a steak or fillet and brush with oil. Broil or grill about 3 inches from heat (4 minutes on each side for rare; 6 minutes on each side for medium; 8 minutes on each side for well-done). Place patties on a platter and top each with 1 tablespoon butter. Serves four.

ENTRECOTE A LA DIANE
(STEAK DIANE FLAMBE)

1 beef sirloin steak, 12 ounces

salt and pepper to taste

1½ teaspoons vegetable oil

4 teaspoons butter

2 medium-sized mushrooms, thinly sliced

4 shallots or 1 small onion, peeled and chopped

2 tablespoons brandy

1 tablespoon A-1 sauce

½ teaspoon Worcestershire sauce

¼ cup dry sherry

½ teaspoon peeled, chopped chives

1 teaspoon chopped, fresh parsley

¼ cup melted butter

Lay steak between two sheets of wax paper and pound it with a meat mallet to a thickness of ¼ inch. Dust steak with salt and pepper and rub lightly with oil. Heat a 9-inch skillet over high heat, and brown steak quickly on both sides. (It is essential to maintain a rare center.) Remove meat to a platter. Place 4 teaspoons of the butter in the skillet. Add mushrooms and shallots. Cook over medium heat until lightly browned, and move them to one side of skillet. Return steak to skillet, add brandy and heat well; flame the brandy and add A-1 sauce, Worcestershire sauce, sherry, chives, parsley, and melted butter. Stir gently to mix. Turn steak over in mixture and serve immediately. Serves one.

PEPPER STEAK

2 tablespoons cracked pepper

4 beef sirloin steaks, 10 ounces each

2 tablespoons vegetable oil

2 tablespoons lemon juice

6 tablespoons butter

1 garlic clove, peeled, crushed, and chopped

1 tablespoon peeled, chopped shallots

½ cup dry red wine

1 tablespoon chopped, fresh parsley

salt and pepper to taste

Press pepper into both sides of steaks with the heel of the hand. Sprinkle with 1 tablespoon of the oil and 1 tablespoon of the lemon juice. Heat remaining 1 tablespoon oil in a 9-inch skillet. Brown steaks over moderately high heat, 3 minutes each side. Place steaks on a heated platter. Add 1 tablespoon of the butter to the skillet; add garlic and shallots, and sauté until golden brown. Add wine and reduce to one-third its volume. Remove skillet from heat and add remaining 5 tablespoons butter, the remaining 1 tablespoon lemon juice, and parsley. Add salt and pepper to taste. Pour sauce over steaks. Serves four.

This dish offers a chance for the hostess to assemble the meal ahead of time and then let the guests do most of the cooking.

FONDUE BOURGUIGNONNE
(BURGUNDY BEEF FONDUE)

1 pound lean beef (fillet or sirloin)

2 cups peanut oil

choice of sauces

Cut beef into ¾-inch cubes. Heat oil in a saucepan over moderate heat to very hot (about 400°F. on deep-frying thermometer). Transfer hot oil to a fondue pot placed over its heat source. Each guest is equipped with a special fondue fork. Spear a meat cube and cook it in the hot oil until it is of the desired doneness. Remove from fondue fork to dinner fork. Meat is then dunked into any one of many sauces such as: mustard sauce, mayonnaise, rémoulade, curry sauce, béarnaise sauce, or sweet-and-sour sauce. Serves two.

BOEUF A LA STROGANOFF
(BEEF STROGANOFF)

2 pounds beef tenderloin, cut in thin strips

1 teaspoon paprika

1 teaspoon salt

1 teaspoon pepper

½ cup butter

1/3 cup peeled, chopped shallots

1 cup sliced mushrooms

2 tablespoons flour

½ cup dry white wine

½ cup Brown Stock (see index)

½ cup sour cream

Sprinkle meat with paprika and salt and pepper. Melt ¼ cup of the butter in a 9-inch skillet, and brown meat quickly over high heat. Remove meat and set aside in a warm place. Melt the remaining ¼ cup butter in the skillet; add shallots and cook until brown. Add mushrooms and sauté until all liquid has evaporated. Add flour and mix well. Gradually add wine and Brown Stock. Bring mixture to a boil, stirring constantly, then simmer for 30 minutes. Remove sauce from heat and fold in sour cream. Add the meat to the sauce. Heat to just below boiling and serve immediately. Serves six.

In this dish, a cheese and a tomato sauce combine to add a zesty flavor to simple boiled beef.

BOEUF EN MIROTON
(BEEF MIROTON)

1 cup butter

5 medium onions, peeled and sliced

2 garlic cloves, crushed and chopped

2 tablespoons flour

1/3 cup tomato sauce

1 cup Brown Stock (see index)

1/3 cup wine vinegar

3 pounds boiled or braised beef

½ cup sliced sour pickles

1/3 cup grated Parmesan cheese

Melt butter in a saucepan, and sauté onions and garlic until golden brown. Add flour and brown slightly. Stir in tomato sauce and Brown Stock, and bring to a boil. Let simmer for 30 minutes. Add vinegar and cook until sauce is reduced to a heavy syrupy consistency. Preheat oven to 350°F. Slice beef and arrange evenly with pickles in a shallow baking dish. Pour sauce over beef; sprinkle with cheese, and bake at 350°F. for 30 minutes. Serves six to eight.

VEAL

Veal is the meat of two-and-one-half to three-month-old calves. It is very tender and easy to prepare. I always tell my students at The Greenbrier Culinary School *never* to overcook veal. It toughens the delicate meat. The texture of veal is so absorbent that herbs, wines, or butter used to flavor it must be measured carefully to insure the very finest taste.

Like beef, veal is divided into grades. Prime is, naturally, outstanding, but choice is also of fine quality and sufficient for almost all veal dishes. Lower grades may require more care and time in preparation, but generally these grades, unlike lower grades of beef, are acceptable. Veal may be purchased in the same cuts as beef.

A favorite on The Greenbrier menu.

RIS DE VEAU AU CHAMPAGNE POLIGNAC
(SWEETBREADS IN CHAMPAGNE SAUCE POLIGNAC)

2 pounds veal sweetbreads

1 teaspoon salt

1/3 cup all-purpose flour

¼ teaspoon each, salt and pepper

1/3 cup butter

1 cup champagne

½ cup heavy cream

1 cup Sauce Supreme (see index)

juice of 1 lemon

2 tablespoons chopped truffles or morels

*½ cup sliced mushrooms
sautéed in 1 tablespoon butter*

In a saucepan, cover sweetbreads with boiling water; add 1 teaspoon salt, cover and simmer 5 minutes. Drain sweetbreads; plunge them into cold running water, and with the fingers, slip off the thin outside membrane. Cut away any dark veins and thick, connective tissue. Combine flour and salt and pepper in a shallow dish. Melt butter in a saucepan. When butter foams, roll sweetbreads in flour mixture and place in the butter. Sauté until uniformly golden brown. Pour off excess butter; add champagne; reduce to one half its volume. Add cream and bring to a boil. Add Sauce Supreme and simmer for 40 minutes. Remove sweetbreads from sauce and place in a shallow dish. Strain sauce, add lemon juice, truffles or morels, and mushrooms and simmer for 5 minutes longer. Pour sauce over sweetbreads. Serves six.

Also called cordon bleu, this is a classic dish that is served the world over.

DOUBLE ESCALOPES DE VEAU METROPOLE
(DOUBLE VEAL CUTLETS METROPOLE)

1 pound veal cut in 8 slices

4 thin slices ham

4 1-ounce slices Gruyère cheese

½ teaspoon each, salt and pepper

2 tablespoons flour

3 eggs, beaten with 1 teaspoon water

1 cup fine, dry bread crumbs

½ cup butter

8 hot, cooked asparagus spears

*4 tablespoons Hollandaise Sauce
(see index), heated*

With a meat mallet, pound cutlets very thin. Cover half the cutlets with a slice of ham and a slice of cheese and then with another slice of veal. Season with salt and pepper. Dust double cutlets with flour and carefully dip first in eggs and then in bread crumbs. Melt butter in a large skillet, and sauté cutlets slowly over low heat until golden on both sides. Take care when turning them that melting cheese does not escape. Cooking time is about 4 minutes on each side. Place cutlets on platter, and put 2 spears of asparagus on each cutlet. Pour 1 tablespoon Hollandaise Sauce over asparagus. Serves four.

A special Italian flavor for veal.

COTES DE VEAU MILANAISE
(VEAL CHOPS MILANESE)

6 veal chops, with bone left on

½ teaspoon each, salt and pepper

2 tablespoons flour

2 eggs

2 tablespoons water

1 cup fine dry bread crumbs

1/3 cup Parmesan cheese

½ cup butter plus 2 teaspoons plus 1 tablespoon

½ pound macaroni

1 tablespoon vegetable oil

2 tablespoons peeled, chopped shallots

1 garlic clove, crushed and chopped

½ cup dry white wine

½ cup tomato purée

1 cup Brown Sauce (see index)

½ cup julienne-cut ham

½ cup julienne-cut mushrooms

½ cup grated Parmesan cheese

½ cup chopped truffles (morels may be substituted)

With a meat mallet, flatten chops to ½-inch thickness. (Hold it by the bone as you flatten.) Season with salt and pepper, and dust with flour. Beat eggs with the water. Mix bread crumbs with

Parmesan cheese. Dip chops first in egg, and then in crumb mixture. Melt ½ cup of the butter in a skillet, and sauté chops over medium heat until a golden color on each side (about four minutes per side). Remove from heat and keep warm. Cook macaroni in boiling, salted water according to package directions. Drain and rinse with warm water. Stir in oil. Put macaroni in a serving bowl, and keep warm. Heat 2 teaspoons of the butter in a saucepan, and sauté shallots and garlic until golden brown. Add white wine, and, over moderate heat, reduce to half its volume. Add tomato purée and Brown Sauce; bring to a boil. Simmer for 5 minutes; meanwhile, sauté ham and mushrooms in the remaining tablespoon butter in a skillet. Add to sauce. Pour sauce over macaroni; sprinkle with Parmesan cheese; top with truffles or morels, and serve with chops. Serves six.

SCALLOPINI DI VITELLO ALLA MARSALA
(VEAL SCALLOPINI MARSALA)

20 small slices veal fillet
(approximately 2 pounds)

½ teaspoon each, salt and pepper

2 tablespoons flour

½ cup butter

½ cup Marsala

juice of 1 lemon

With a meat mallet, pound pieces of veal very flat. Season them with salt and pepper, and dust with flour. Melt butter in a 9-inch skillet, and sauté veal quickly over moderately high heat. Drain off any excess butter, and add Marsala wine to the veal. Bring to a boil. Arrange scallopini on a platter, mix lemon juice with the drippings, and pour drippings on top of meat. Serves four.

Time and effort are involved in this entrée, but the results are worthwhile.

FRICASSEE DE VEAU A L'ANCIENNE
(VEAL STEW IN WHITE SAUCE)

4 pounds boneless veal shoulder

1 teaspoon salt

½ teaspoon pepper

½ cup butter

1 large onion, peeled and chopped

1 carrot, scraped and chopped

1 celery stalk, chopped

1 garlic clove, peeled and crushed

juice of 1 lemon

3 tablespoons flour

½ cup dry white wine

1 cup White Stock (see index)

1 spice bag (1 bay leaf, 2 cloves, and 2 sprigs
marjoram tied in cheesecloth)

1 bouquet garni (1 bay leaf, 1 sprig fresh thyme, and
2 sprigs fresh parsley tied in cheesecloth)

salt and pepper to taste

dash of nutmeg

16 medium-sized mushrooms,
sautéed in 1 tablespoon butter

16 peeled pearl onions,
cooked 10 minutes in boiling water

½ cup heavy cream

Preheat oven to 300°F. Cut veal into 1½-inch cubes. Put cubes in a 4-quart saucepan, and cover with cold water. Bring to a boil and simmer 5 minutes. Then drain and dry on paper towels. Sprinkle with salt and pepper. Melt butter in a 4-quart, ovenproof casserole, and sauté veal until golden brown. Add onion, carrots, celery, garlic, and lemon juice. Cook until onion is transparent. Sprinkle mixture with flour; mix well and cook for 5 minutes. Add wine and White Stock, and bring to a boil. Add spice bag and bouquet garni. Cover and bake at 300°F. for 1½ hours. When done, remove and discard spice bag and bouquet garni. With a slotted spoon, remove meat from sauce, piece by piece, and place it in a bowl. Strain sauce through a sieve into a 4-quart saucepan, and bring to a boil. Add salt and pepper to taste and nutmeg. Add meat, mushrooms, and pearl onions to sauce. Simmer 10 minutes. Then fold in cream. Serve in a large bowl. Serves eight.

Veal cooked in white wine is a delightful and delicate dish.

EMINCE DE VEAU
(MINCED VEAL)

1½ pounds boneless veal from leg

¼ teaspoon each, salt and pepper

1/3 cup butter

2 tablespoons flour

1 onion, peeled and chopped

1 cup dry white wine

½ cup Brown Sauce (see index)

juice of 1 lemon

Cut veal in small slivers and sprinkle with salt and pepper. Melt half the butter in a large skillet, and sauté veal quickly over moderately high heat. Sprinkle with flour, mix well and remove veal from pan to a platter. Melt the remaining butter in skillet and sauté onions until golden brown. Add wine and reduce to one half its volume. Add Brown Sauce and bring to a boil. Add sautéed veal and lemon juice and again bring to a boil. Add salt and pepper to taste. Serves four.

The delicate taste of the veal comes through the spices.

PICCATINI DI VITELLO
(SLICES OF VEAL)

1 pound veal leg cut into 12 small slices

3 eggs

¼ cup grated Parmesan cheese

1 teaspoon dried thyme leaves

1 teaspoon dried oregano leaves

¼ teaspoon each, salt and pepper

2 tablespoons flour

½ cup butter

With a meat mallet, pound veal slices very flat. Beat eggs slightly, and mix in cheese, thyme, oregano, salt and pepper. Dust veal slices with flour and dip them into egg mixture. Melt butter in a large skillet and add veal slices. Brown on each side over low heat. Arrange veal on serving plate and serve with Saffron Rice (see index). Serves four.

Veal kidneys are a longstanding favorite food in France, and this recipe is also popular at The Greenbrier.

ROGNONS DE VEAU GREENBRIER
(VEAL KIDNEYS GREENBRIER)

4 veal kidneys

½ teaspoon each, salt and pepper

¼ teaspoon dried thyme leaves

4 tablespoons butter

2 tablespoons peeled, chopped shallots

1 cup dried morels, soaked in lukewarm water

1 cup dry white wine

1 cup heavy cream

1 teaspoon Meat Glaze (see index)

juice of 1 lemon

2 tablespoons brandy

8 toasted bread croutons, cut into heart shapes

2 tablespoons melted butter

Trim fat from kidneys. Scald in boiling water for two minutes. Rinse in cold water. Remove skin. Cut kidneys into quarters. Cut out and discard white veins and hard portions. Slice kidneys in thin slivers. Season with salt, pepper, and thyme. Melt the 4 tablespoons butter in a skillet, and sauté kidneys for 2 minutes. Spoon them out onto a heated platter. Add shallots to skillet and let them brown over medium heat. Add drained morels and heat them well. Add white wine and reduce to half its volume. Add cream and Meat Glaze and bring to a boil. Reduce heat and simmer for 5 minutes. Add kidneys and lemon juice. Again, bring to a boil. Put mixture in serving dish and sprinkle brandy over top. Brush toasted croutons with the melted butter and place on top. Serves four.

LAMB

"America is a beef nation," according to many people, but lamb is on the menu at The Greenbrier at almost every meal and is ordered by scores of people every day.

Baby lamb, which is rarely available in grocery stores, is milk-fed and is considered a delicacy. It has less flavor than the three-to-six-month-old spring lamb, which I consider the best. From six months to one-year-old lamb is still excellent. As a lamb ages, it acquires layers of fat that change its flavor drastically. Spring lamb still has marbling throughout, making it tender and flavorful.

As with veal, it is very important never to overcook lamb. It should be served when slightly pink in color. Most of my recipes, which have been perfected in Europe, include wines, herbs, and vegetables. The European influence in these recipes is understandable because Europeans consider lamb a delicate and elegant meat.

Served with chutney and rice, this makes a wonderful dinner dish.

CURRIE D'AGNEAU A L'INDIENNE
(INDIAN LAMB CURRY)

4 pounds boneless lamb shoulder

½ teaspoon each, salt and pepper

3 tablespoons butter

3 garlic cloves, peeled, crushed, and chopped

2 large onions, peeled and chopped

1 tablespoon curry powder

2 tablespoons flour

½ cup peeled, diced apples

2 tablespoons tomato purée

½ cup dry white wine

2 cups Chicken Broth (see index)

1 bouquet garni (1 bay leaf, 2 sprigs fresh parsley, 1 sprig fresh thyme tied in cheesecloth bag)

½ cup heavy cream

3 cups hot, cooked rice

Preheat oven to 350°F. Cut lamb into 1-inch squares. Season with ½ teaspoon salt and ½ teaspoon pepper. Melt butter in large saucepan, and sauté the lamb until golden brown. Add garlic and onions, and sauté until onions are transparent. Sprinkle curry and flour over lamb mixture; mix well, and sauté 3 minutes longer. Add apples, tomato purée, wine, Chicken Broth, and bouquet garni. Bring to a boil and skim off fat. Turn mixture into a 2½-3-quart casserole. Cover and bake at 350°F. for 1½ hours. Remove casserole from oven, and discard bouquet garni. Fold in cream. Season to taste with salt and pepper. Serve with rice. Serves six to eight.

Along with Andalouse Compote and rice, this highly seasoned dish is reminiscent of the cooking of southern Europe.

GIGOT D'AGNEAU ROTI ANDALOUSE
(ROAST LEG OF LAMB ANDALOUSE)

1 leg of lamb, weighing about 6 pounds

2 garlic cloves, peeled and crushed

½ teaspoon each, salt and pepper

2 tablespoons vegetable oil

2 tablespoons dried rosemary leaves

2 tablespoons bacon fat

½ cup peeled, chopped onion

¼ cup chopped celery

½ cup diced ham (or bacon)

2 small carrots, scraped and coarsely chopped

1 sprig fresh thyme

1 bay leaf

½ cup dry red wine

½ cup Brown Stock (see index)

*1 tablespoon cornstarch
mixed with 1 teaspoon water*

1½ cups Andalouse Compote (see index)

Preheat oven to 325°F. Rub lamb with garlic; season with ½ teaspoon salt and ½ teaspoon pepper; brush with oil, and sprinkle with rosemary. Melt bacon fat in roasting pan in the oven. Remove pan from oven. Roll lamb leg in the hot fat to coat it evenly. Roast at 325°F. for 25 minutes on each side, basting frequently with pan juices. Add onions, celery, ham (or bacon), carrots, thyme, and bay leaf. (This may be in the form of a *mirepoix* and tied together in a cheesecloth bag.) Roast uncovered for another 30 minutes, basting often. Allow 18 to 20 minutes per pound cooking time. When done, remove lamb to a platter (allow lamb to set 15 minutes before carving). Drain fat from roasting pan, and pour drippings into a saucepan. Add wine and Brown Stock and simmer for 15 minutes. Strain and return gravy to saucepan. Bring to a boil and stir in cornstarch-water mixture. Bring to a boil. Season to taste with salt and pepper. Serve with Andalouse Compote. Serves six.

Two racks of lamb, tied together to form a crown roast, provide a showpiece for guests.

COURONNE D'AGNEAU ROTIE
(CROWN OF LAMB ROAST)

2 racks of lamb (12 chops)

1 garlic clove, peeled and crushed

½ teaspoon each, salt and pepper

4 tablespoons vegetable oil

1 tablespoon dried rosemary leaves

½ cup peeled, chopped onions

¼ cup chopped celery

½ cup diced ham

2 small carrots, scraped and chopped

1 sprig fresh thyme

1 bay leaf

½ cup dry white wine

½ cup Brown Stock (see index)

*2 teaspoons cornstarch
mixed with 2 teaspoons water*

Preheat oven to 400°F. Tie lamb racks together in the shape of a crown. Rub with garlic; season with salt and pepper; brush with oil, and sprinkle with rosemary. Place lamb in a shallow roasting pan. Roast at 400°F. for 30 minutes. Lower oven temperature to 375°F. and roast 15 minutes longer. Add onions, celery, ham, carrots, thyme and bay leaf to pan and cook until onions are brown. Remove meat to a platter. Drain off fat from roasting pan and pour drippings into a saucepan. Add wine and Brown Stock and simmer for 5 minutes. Strain and return gravy to saucepan. Add cornstarch mixture. Bring to a boil and skim off fat. Season to taste with salt and pepper. Serve gravy with lamb. Serves four.

The less lamb kidney is cooked, the more tender it is.

ROGNONS D'AGNEAU AU COGNAC
(LAMB KIDNEYS WITH COGNAC)

8 lamb kidneys

3 teaspoons butter

¼ teaspoon each, salt and pepper

¼ teaspoon allspice

1 tablespoon flour

1 tablespoon onions, peeled and chopped

1 tablespoon flour

½ cup dry white wine

½ cup Brown Stock (see index)

½ tablespoon Meat Glaze (see index)

1/3 cup cognac

hot, cooked rice or buttered toast

Preheat oven to 350°F. Trim fat from kidneys. Scald in boiling water for 3 minutes. Rinse in cold water. Remove skin; cut kidneys into quarters. Cut out and discard white veins and hard portions. Melt butter in a saucepan with ovenproof handle. Add kidneys, ¼ teaspoon salt, ¼ teaspoon pepper, and allspice; sprinkle with the 1 tablespoon flour. Sauté kidneys until golden brown. Add onion, and sauté until it is transparent. Sprinkle with remaining 1 tablespoon flour. Mix well; add wine and Brown Stock and Meat Glaze, and bring to a boil. Cover and bake at 350°F. for 10 minutes. Remove from oven. Add cognac, and season to taste with salt and pepper. Serve on rice or hot buttered toast. Serves four.

This is one of the most exquisite pieces of lamb you can serve.

CARRE D'AGNEAU PERSILLADE
(RACK OF LAMB PERSILLADE)

2 racks of lamb, 6 chops each

1 teaspoon each, salt and pepper

1 tablespoon dried rosemary leaves

2 tablespoons vegetable oil

2 tablespoons chopped, fresh parsley

3 tablespoons fine, dry bread crumbs

1 garlic clove, peeled, crushed, and chopped

½ teaspoon dry mustard

2 egg yolks, slightly beaten

½ cup peeled, chopped onion

¼ cup chopped celery

½ cup diced ham

1 sprig fresh thyme

1 bay leaf

½ cup dry white wine

½ cup Brown Stock (see index)

*2 tablespoons cornstarch
mixed with 1 tablespoon water*

Preheat oven to 450°F. Place lamb, fat side down, in roasting pan. Sprinkle lamb with 1 teaspoon salt, 1 teaspoon pepper, rosemary, and oil. Roast uncovered at 450°F. for 15 minutes. Mix parsley, bread crumbs, garlic, mustard, and eggs (this is called *persillade*), and apply to surface of lamb as a coating. Bake for 20 minutes more. Add onions, celery, ham, thyme, and bay leaf to pan, and cook until onions turn brown — about 20 minutes. Remove lamb to a platter. Drain fat from roasting pan, and pour drippings into a saucepan. Add wine and Brown Stock and simmer for 5 minutes. Strain and return gravy to saucepan. Add cornstarch-water mixture. Bring to a boil and skim off fat. Season to taste with salt and pepper. Serve gravy with lamb. Serves four.

A favorite Middle Eastern dish with an American flair.

BROCHETTE D'AGNEAU CAUCASIENNE
(SHISH KEBAB CAUCASIAN)

3 pounds boneless leg of lamb

½ cup red wine

½ cup vegetable oil

1 tablespoon peeled, chopped shallots

1 bay leaf

1 garlic clove, peeled, crushed, and chopped

2 tablespoons lemon juice

1 tablespoon dried thyme leaves

6 mushrooms, halved

2 tablespoons butter plus ½ cup soft butter

12 squares, 1-inch each, green pepper,
blanched in boiling water

3 firm, unpeeled tomatoes, quartered

3 onions, peeled and quartered

2 tablespoons olive oil

1 teaspoon dried tarragon leaves

salt and pepper to taste

2 cups Saffron Rice (see index)

Cut lamb into 1-inch cubes and put in a deep bowl. Make marinade by combining wine, vegetable oil, shallots, bay leaf, garlic, lemon juice, and thyme. Pour marinade over lamb cubes. Cover and let stand in refrigerator for 1½ hours. Before cooking, drain lamb thoroughly. Sauté mushrooms in 2 tablespoons butter until lightly browned. Thread each of six skewers alternately with mushrooms, lamb cubes, pepper, tomato, and onion, pressed closely together. Brush brochettes with olive oil, and arrange them on a broiler rack. Preheat broiler and place brochettes 3 to 4 inches from heat. Broil about 8 minutes, turning occasionally to brown all sides. Remove brochettes to a warm serving platter. Mix together the ½ cup soft butter and the tarragon. Spread each brochette with some of the mixture. Sprinkle with salt and pepper to taste. Serve with Saffron Rice. Serves six.

PORK

Someone once said that everything from the pig can be used save the whistle. This comes quite close to being true. Rendered pork fat is used by professional chefs in cakes and pastries because of its delicate flavor; the meat, which is available in the same cuts as beef, lamb, and veal, is also a source of bacon, sausage, ham, shoulder, pork knuckles, pig's feet, and head cheese.

The flavor of pork blends well with all vegetables, and it is particularly good with stronger flavored vegetables such as beans, sauerkraut, and cabbage. Its flavor is brought out by apples, oranges, prunes, and other fruits, as well as by brown sugar.

Most pork dishes are at their best when cooked for a relatively long time at a low temperature.

Served with red cabbage and apple sauce, this roast pork dish is a delightful luncheon or supper item.

CARRE DE PORC ROTI NORMANDE
(ROAST PORK NORMANDE)

1 loin of pork, 4 to 5 pounds

½ teaspoon each, salt and pepper

½ cup peeled, chopped onions

¼ cup chopped celery

½ cup diced ham

2 small carrots, scraped and chopped

1 sprig fresh thyme

1 bay leaf

½ cup apple cider

1 cup Brown Stock (see index)

*1 tablespoon cornstarch
mixed with 1 tablespoon water*

5 apples, peeled and sliced

2 tablespoons butter

Preheat oven to 425°F. Season pork with ½ teaspoon salt and ½ teaspoon pepper. Put in roasting pan, fat side down, and roast at 425°F. for 20 minutes. Turn roast; lower heat to 325°F., and add onions, celery, ham, carrots, thyme, and bay leaf. Roast for 1½ hours, basting frequently with pan drippings. Remove and place pork on serving platter. Drain fat from roasting pan, and pour drippings into a saucepan. Add cider and cook for 3 minutes over medium heat. Add Brown Stock and bring to a boil. Add cornstarch mixture and simmer for 10 minutes. Strain and skim off fat. Season to taste with salt and pepper. Serve gravy with pork. Sauté sliced apples in heated butter in a skillet until lightly browned, and serve on platter with sliced pork. Serves six.

A marvelous luncheon dish when served with the traditional Milanese dish of macaroni.

COTES DE PORC A LA MILANAISE
(PORK CHOPS MILANESE)

6 pork chops, 1-inch thick

¼ teaspoon each, salt and pepper

2 tablespoons flour

3 eggs, beaten with 2 tablespoons water

½ cup fine, dry bread crumbs

1/3 cup grated Parmesan cheese

½ cup butter

With a meat mallet, flatten chops to ½-inch thickness. Sprinkle with salt and pepper and dust with flour. Dip first in egg mixture, then in bread crumbs to which the grated cheese has been added. Melt butter in skillet, and sauté chops slowly over low heat until golden brown on both sides. Serve with your favorite pasta. Serves six.

Garnished with the fruits of the Easter season, ham is a special holiday treat.

JAMBON DE PAQUES
(EASTER HAM)

1 country-style ham, 12 pounds

water to cover

½ cup firmly packed brown sugar

10 pineapple rings

10 dried, pitted prunes

½ pound pignolia nuts

2 cups port

Preheat oven to 325°F. Cover ham with water in a roasting pan. Cover and bake at 325°F. for 6 hours. Drain off water and rub ham with brown sugar. Return to oven until sugar melts (a few minutes). Secure pineapple and prunes with toothpicks in a decorative fashion on the ham. Crush the pignolia nuts and mix with brown sugar. Sprinkle them on the fruits. Sprinkle port over top and continue to bake for 30 minutes.

Note: If a fully cooked (bone-in) ham is used, omit water and bake uncovered for 4 hours.

A festive and attractive dinner item.

COTES DE PORC FARCIE HAWAIIAN
(STUFFED PORK CHOPS HAWAIIAN)

6 double pork chops, 1-inch thick

6 tablespoons chopped mushrooms

1 tablespoon chopped onions

2 tablespoons chopped, fresh parsley

2 tablespoons fine, dry bread crumbs

1 teaspoon dried thyme leaves

1 egg, slightly beaten

¼ teaspoon each, salt and pepper

1/3 cup all-purpose flour

1/3 cup butter plus 2 tablespoons butter

¾ cup dry white wine

1/3 cup pineapple juice

½ cup Brown Sauce (see index)

6 pineapple slices

Preheat oven to 375°F. Slit open a pocket next to the bone in each chop. Mix mushrooms, onions, parsley, bread crumbs, thyme, egg, ¼ teaspoon salt and ¼ teaspoon pepper together. Put 2 tablespoons of the filling in each pocket. Dip stuffed chops in flour. Melt the 1/3 cup butter in a skillet with ovenproof handle, and slowly brown chops on both sides until golden brown. Drain off half of the fat and add the wine and the Brown Sauce. Cover and bake at 375°F. for 30 minutes. Arrange chops on platter and keep warm. Add pineapple juice to skillet and simmer over low heat for 20 minutes. Season to taste with salt and pepper. Melt the remaining 2 tablespoons butter in a skillet, and lightly brown pineapple slices. Put one slice on each chop. Ladle sauce over chops. Serves six.

A wonderful entrée for special parties or at a buffet.

LE COCHON DE LAIT FARCI
(STUFFED SUCKLING PIG)

1 suckling pig, 10 to 15 pounds

2 tablespoons dried thyme leaves

½ cup mushrooms

2 tablespoons minced onions

1 cup peeled, diced apples

2 tablespoons butter

½ cup dry bread crumbs

2 eggs, slightly beaten

½ teaspoon nutmeg

½ teaspoon salt

½ teaspoon pepper

½ cup melted bacon fat

½ cup peeled and chopped onions

¼ cup chopped celery

½ cup diced ham

2 small carrots, scraped and chopped

1 sprig fresh thyme

1 bay leaf

1/3 cup dry mustard
mixed with 3 tablespoons water

1 red apple

½ cup apple cider

½ cup Brown Stock (see index)

1 tablespoon cornstarch
mixed with 1 teaspoon water

Wash suckling pig thoroughly inside and out. Dry with paper towels and sprinkle thyme in cavity. Place in refrigerator for 12 hours. Preheat oven to 350°F. Mix mushrooms, onion, and diced apples that have been sautéed in the 2 tablespoons butter with the bread crumbs and eggs, and season with nutmeg. Sprinkle cavity of pig with ½ teaspoon salt and ½ teaspoon pepper. Fill with the stuffing mixture. With skewers and string, lace opening closed. Cover snout, ears, and tail with foil to protect them from burning. Pull hindlegs backward and forelegs forward and tie securely. Put bacon fat in a large roasting pan and add onions, celery, ham, carrots, thyme, and bay leaf (may be added in form of a *mirepoix* tied together in cheesecloth). Set pig on bed of vegetables of your own choice. Roast at 350°F. for 5 hours, basting every 10 minutes or so with drippings in pan. For crisp skin and spicy tang, brush pig with mustard every 15 minutes. When done, remove pig to large platter, and put whole red apple in the mouth. Drain fat from pan and pour drippings into a saucepan. Add cider, Brown Stock, and cornstarch-water mixture. Simmer for 10 minutes. Strain gravy into another saucepan; bring to a boil, and add any remaining mustard paste. Season to taste with salt and pepper. Serve sauce in side dish. Serves eight to ten.

GAME

The term *game* applies to all wild animals and birds that are hunted for food. It includes small birds, such as quail, lark, pigeon, dove, and woodcock; large birds, such as turkey, pheasant, prairie hen, grouse, and duck; small game, such as rabbit, squirrel, woodchuck; and large game, such as deer, bear, elk, and moose.

A long cooking time is generally required for game. Small quantities of wine are usually used in preparing small birds, while heavy spices are generally reserved for larger birds. Cheeses, onions, and sherry enhance small game, and long cooking periods, proper spices, and vegetables bring out the best flavor of any of the large game.

Since game is not readily available in markets, you may have to find special suppliers for it or hunt it yourself. It is well worth the effort it may take to obtain it and cook it.

155

SELLE DE CHEVREUIL GRAND VENEUR
(SADDLE OF VENISON GRAND VENEUR)

To prepare venison

1 saddle of venison, 4 to 5 pounds

1½ teaspoons salt

1 teaspoon pepper

Marinade

1 cup dry red wine

½ cup red wine vinegar

½ cup water

2 tablespoons vegetable oil

2 sprigs fresh parsley

2 garlic cloves, peeled and crushed

8 juniper berries

2 whole cloves

1 bay leaf

1 sprig fresh thyme

2 onions, peeled and sliced

1 carrot, scraped and sliced

1 stalk celery, sliced

To cook venison

1/3 cup melted butter

½ cup brandy, warmed

1 cup Brown Stock (see index)

2 tablespoons currant jelly

1/3 cup sour cream

salt and pepper to taste

Remove skin from venison and sprinkle with salt and pepper. Combine all ingredients for marinade and simmer 30 minutes. Place venison in a deep dish and cover with marinade. Cover and let stand in refrigerator for 3 to 4 days, turning from time to time. When ready to cook, preheat oven to 450°F. Remove venison from marinade. Spread the marinade on the bottom of a roasting pan; add venison, and brush with melted butter. Roast at 450°F. for 30 minutes. Reduce oven temperature to 325°F. Continue to roast venison, allowing 10 minutes cooking time per pound. Baste frequently. When done, remove venison to warm platter. Drain drippings from roasting pan into a 1-quart measuring cup. Skim off fat. Add warm brandy to roasting pan and ignite. Pour in 2 cups of the drippings. Return roasting pan to oven for 10 minutes. Add Brown Stock and cook 10 minutes longer in oven. Strain sauce into a saucepan and bring to a boil. Skim off any fat. Add currant jelly and sour cream. Add salt and pepper to taste. Serve sauce separately. Buttered noodles will complement this dish. Serves four.

Roast duck is delicious, and in this recipe it is done in a crisp, relatively dry fashion.

CANETON ROTI CHINOISE
(CHINESE ROAST DUCK)

Marinade

4 teaspoons Chicken Broth (see index)

4 teaspoons soy sauce

4 teaspoons honey

1 teaspoon grated orange peel

1 teaspoon sugar

1 teaspoon salt

1 teaspoon cinnamon

½ teaspoon anise seed, crushed

4 teaspoons vinegar

Game

1 ready-to-cook duck, 4 to 5 pounds

1 teaspoon salt

½ teaspoon pepper

juice of 1 orange

1/3 cup saki wine

1/3 cup Chicken Broth (see index)

½ teaspoon cornstarch mixed with
1 teaspoon water

In a large bowl, mix all ingredients for the marinade. Wash duck and trim off any excess skin. Season inside with salt and pepper. Place duck in the marinade, and let stand at room temperature 1 hour, turning duck occasionally. Preheat oven to 350°F. Remove duck from marinade and place it in a roasting pan. Add 1 cup water to pan. Roast uncovered at 350°F. for 2 hours, basting frequently with the marinade and turning occasionally. Remove duck from oven and place on a serving platter. Drain fat from roasting pan and pour drippings into a saucepan. Add orange juice, saki, Chicken Broth, and any remaining marinade; bring to a boil. Stir in cornstarch-water mixture and simmer for 2 minutes. Strain and serve sauce with carved duck. Serves four.

PERDREAU VERONIQUE
(PARTRIDGE VERONIQUE)

4 young, ready-to-cook, partridges (quail)

½ teaspoon each, salt and pepper

½ teaspoon dried thyme leaves

8 slices bacon

2/3 cup melted butter

2/3 cup brandy, warmed

2/3 cup dry white wine

1 cup Game Stock (see index)

*2 teaspoons cornstarch mixed with
2 teaspoons water*

2/3 cup curaçao

2 cups seedless green grapes

Preheat oven to 450°F. Season birds inside and out with salt, pepper, and thyme. Cover breasts with bacon slices, and tie wings and legs securely to body. Arrange in a roasting pan, side by side.

Brush generously with butter. Roast uncovered at 450°F. for 15 minutes. Drain off fat from roasting pan. Add brandy and ignite. When flames die down, add wine and Game Stock. Return birds to oven and roast 20 minutes longer, basting occasionally. Place birds on platter. Strain sauce into a saucepan. Skim off residue from top. Stir in constarch-water mixture and simmer for 2 minutes. Add curaçao. Add grapes. Add salt and pepper to taste, and ladle sauce over partridges. Serves four.

A delightful way to serve the smallest edible bird.

CAILLES AU RIZOTTO
(QUAIL WITH RICE)

8 young, ready-to-cook, partridges (quail)

½ teaspoon each, salt and pepper

8 strips bacon

½ cup butter

1/3 cup peeled, chopped shallots

1 garlic clove, crushed and chopped

1/3 cup dry white wine

1 cup Brown Stock (see index)

*2 tablespoons quick-cooking tapioca,
mixed with 1 tablespoon water*

2 tablespoons brandy

2 cups cooked Wild Rice (see index)

2 truffles or morels, chopped

Preheat oven to 450°F. Season quail inside and out with salt and pepper. Tie a bacon strip around each quail and tie wings and legs securely to body. Arrange them in a large skillet with an ovenproof handle. Brush generously with butter, and brown quail quickly over high heat, turning to brown all sides. Put skillet in oven and roast at 450°F. for 12 minutes. Transfer quail to serving platter and keep hot. Drain two-thirds of the fat from skillet and sauté shallots and garlic until golden brown. Add white wine, Brown Stock, and tapioca. Simmer 5 minutes. Strain sauce into a saucepan; bring to a boil, and skim fat off surface. Simmer for 10 minutes. Add salt and pepper to taste. Add brandy. Serve gravy and quail with Wild Rice to which truffles or morels have been added. Serves eight.

Breast of pheasant is served under glass to hold in the cognac flavor that makes this dish so unique.

SUPREME DE FAISAN SOUS CLOCHE MAISON
(BREAST OF PHEASANT UNDER GLASS)

2 pheasant breasts

2 tablespoons lemon juice

½ teaspoon salt

½ teaspoon pepper

3 tablespoons butter

1 teaspoon peeled, chopped shallots

2 tablespoons brandy

1/3 cup dry white wine

½ cup heavy cream

1 tablespoon Meat Glaze (see index)

dash of cayenne

1 tablespoon truffles or morels,
cut into thin strips

2 tablespoons mushrooms, cut in thin strips

Remove the skin from the breasts. Trim edges and flatten breasts slightly with a meat mallet. Rub breasts with 1 tablespoon of the lemon juice, and sprinkle with salt and pepper. Melt 2 tablespoons of the butter in a 9-inch skillet. When butter foams, add breasts and sauté 3 minutes on each side. Do not overcook. Make a shallow cut in one of the breasts with a sharp knife. The meat should be pink and the juices that run out should be clear yellow. Remove breasts from skillet and keep warm. Add shallots to drippings and sauté until golden brown. Drain butter from shallots and reserve. Add brandy and wine and reduce to half its volume. Add cream and Meat Glaze and reduce to half its volume again. Strain sauce, and add the remaining 1 tablespoon lemon juice, the remaining tablespoon butter and cayenne. Mix truffles (or morels) and mushrooms, and divide into two portions. Place warm breasts on a serving dish. Top each with truffles and mushrooms. Pour sauce over breasts, and cover with a glass cover. Serves two.

This American holiday favorite, a gift from the Pilgrims, has won great appeal throughout Europe.

DINDE FARCIE AUX MARRONS
(ROAST TURKEY WITH CHESTNUT STUFFING)

Turkey

1 turkey (16 to 18 pounds)

2 teaspoons salt

1½ teaspoons pepper

2 tablespoons allspice

4 stalks celery, sliced thickly

½ cup bacon drippings

Stuffing

½ cup chopped, peeled onions

2 garlic cloves, peeled, crushed, and chopped

½ cup butter

½ cup sausage meat

10 slices bread, toasted and coarsely crumbled

2 cups cooked chopped chestnuts

½ cup brandy

Sauce

1 cup turkey drippings

1 cup dry white wine

2 tablespoons cornstarch

1/3 cup brandy

salt and pepper to taste

1 cup Cranberry Compote (see index)

Preheat oven to 400°F. Wash turkey and pat dry with paper towels. Rub the turkey inside and out with salt, pepper, and allspice. Put celery in body cavity, and tie turkey's legs together. Fasten neck skin to back with a skewer. Fold wing tips onto back. Place turkey on a rack in a large, shallow roasting pan, and brush with bacon drippings. Roast, uncovered, at 400°F. for 25 minutes. Baste frequently with bacon drippings. To prepare stuffing, sauté onions and garlic in melted butter in a skillet until transparent. Add sausage meat and brown well. In a large bowl, combine toasted bread, chestnuts, and sausage mixture. Sprinkle with ½ cup brandy and toss to combine well. Set aside until ready to use. Take turkey from oven, untie legs and discard celery. Fill body cavity loosely with stuffing and close with skewers. Pour off about half the fat from the roasting pan but not the drippings. Place turkey in center of pan, breast side up, and cover loosely with foil. Roast uncovered at 325°F. for 5½ to 6 hours, basting frequently with pan drippings. Turkey is done when the thigh joint moves easily in its socket and the thickest part of the drumstick feels very soft when pressed between protected fingers. A meat thermometer inserted in the thickest part of the thigh should register about 185°F. Transfer turkey to a platter and keep warm. To prepare sauce, skim off and discard fat from drippings in roasting pan. Measure 1 cup of the drippings and pour into a saucepan. Add wine and simmer 10 minutes. In a small bowl, combine cornstarch and the 1/3 cup brandy; add cornstarch mixture to simmering mixture. Cook, stirring constantly, until thickened. Season to taste with salt and pepper. Arrange slices of turkey with stuffing. Serve with sauce and Cranberry Compote. Serves ten to twelve.

LA COMPOTE DE CANNEBERGES
(CRANBERRY COMPOTE)

4 cups fresh cranberries

2 cups sugar

2 cups boiling water

1 tablespoon grated orange peel

peel of 1 lemon

peel of 1 orange

Wash cranberries; remove and discard any stems and soft berries. Put cranberries in a 2-quart saucepan with all the remaining ingredients. Cover loosely and simmer for 15 minutes until cranberries burst. Let cool and discard lemon and orange peels. Serve with turkey or other poultry dishes.

POULTRY

Poultry is universally popular, in the United States, throughout Europe, and in the Orient. Recipes for preparing it are so varied that it can usually successfully appear on a menu several times within a week. Poultry also freezes quite successfully.

The principal types of poultry—limiting the term to the domestic hen or chicken—include broilers and fryers, roasters, capons, and fowls. Broilers and fryers are young chickens of either sex, meaty and tender, suitable for many types of cooking. Roasters are full-grown male chickens with fat-covered carcasses that are often served stuffed with dressing; capons are castrated male chickens that are usually roasted; and fowls are hens past their egg-laying prime, usually reserved for fricasseeing.

Poultry is delicious served hot or cold. It is invaluable in stocks, soups, and sauces. The flavor of poultry is enhanced when it is served with herbs and spices, garlic, onions, shallots, mushrooms, and/or wine. The giblets (liver, heart, and gizzard) are considered a delicacy by many people.

It is little wonder that poultry has such tremendous appeal and is so frequently ordered by The Greenbrier diners.

167

In this recipe, chicken is coated with a rich, smooth sauce. Served in patty shells with a salad and a fresh fruit dessert, it is the perfect summer luncheon dish.

POULET A LA KING
(CHICKEN A LA KING)

2 whole chicken breasts

1/3 cup butter

2 small green peppers, cleaned and cut into strips

½ pound fresh mushrooms, cleaned and quartered

juice of 1 lemon

½ teaspoon each, salt and pepper

3 tablespoons flour

2/3 cup dry sherry

1 cup heavy cream

2 egg yolks, slightly beaten

1 jar pimientos, 4-ounce size, drained and sliced

Simmer chicken breasts in lightly salted water 40 minutes. Remove chicken and cool. Remove meat from bones and cut into cubes. Melt butter in a saucepan; add green peppers, mushrooms, lemon juice, salt and pepper. Sauté until peppers are soft. Add chicken. Sprinkle mixture with flour and mix well. Add 1/3 cup of the sherry and ¾ cup of the cream. Bring to boil then reduce heat and simmer for 5 minutes. Fold in egg yolks mixed with the remaining ¼ cup cream. Stir in the remaining 1/3 cup sherry and pimientos. Adjust seasoning to taste with salt and pepper. Heat gently and serve immediately. Serves six.

This succulent preparation is fit for a czar.

LA POITRINE DE POULARDE A LA KIEV
(CHICKEN KIEV)

*2 whole chicken breasts, skinned,
boned, and halved*

1 cup butter

1 cup chicken livers, cooked and finely chopped

4 tablespoons finely chopped chives

½ teaspoon each, salt and pepper

2/3 cup all-purpose flour

4 eggs, beaten

2 cups, fine, dry bread crumbs

1 cup butter

1 cup vegetable oil

Place chicken breasts between 2 sheets of waxed paper. With a meat mallet, pound each breast to about ¼-inch thickness. Mix the butter with the chopped liver and chopped chives. Divide mixture into four parts, and mold each part into a cylinder. Place one cylinder on each chicken breast, and roll the breast around it, completely enclosing the butter mixture. Sprinkle with salt and pepper. Dip breasts first in flour, then in eggs. Roll them in the bread crumbs to coat evenly. Heat the remaining 1 cup butter with oil in large deep saucepan over medium heat to 360°F. on a deep-frying thermometer. Add breasts and fry until golden brown on all sides, 5 to 8 minutes. Drain on paper towel and serve immediately. Serves four.

A real American delight that can be prepared on the backyard grill or in a kitchen.

BARBECUED CHICKEN

2 broiler-fryer chickens, 2½-pound size, split

½ teaspoon each, salt and pepper

Sauce

½ cup catsup

½ cup Chicken Broth (see index)

2 tablespoons vinegar

1/3 teaspoon each, salt and pepper

½ teaspoon paprika

¼ teaspoon cayenne

¼ teaspoon chili powder

1 teaspoon sugar

1 tablespoon Worcestershire sauce

dash Tabasco sauce

1 tablespoon peeled, chopped shallots

½ cup vegetable oil

1 garlic clove, peeled and chopped

juice of 1 lemon

½ cup butter

¼ cup chopped fresh parsley

1 garlic clove, peeled and chopped
(this is garnish; keep separate from other clove)

Wash chicken and pat dry with paper towels. Season chicken on both sides with ½ teaspoon each of salt and pepper. In a saucepan, combine all ingredients for sauce except parsley and second garlic clove. Bring to a boil. Reduce heat and simmer for 5 minutes. Dip chicken pieces into sauce, and place on charcoal grill or on broiler pan. Grill or broil as manufacturer directs for about 45 minutes or until tender on inside and golden brown on outside. Brush chicken with sauce often, and turn chicken several times while barbecuing. Remove to serving platter and sprinkle with parsley and chopped garlic. Serves four.

POULET SAUTE STANLEY
(CHICKEN STANLEY)

2 broiler-fryer chickens, 3-pound size cut up

1 teaspoon each, salt and pepper

½ teaspoon nutmeg

1 cup milk

¾ cup all-purpose flour

½ cup butter plus 2 tablespoons

1½ cups peeled, sliced onions

2 garlic cloves, peeled, crushed, and chopped

½ cup dry white wine

1 cup heavy cream

1 cup Chicken Broth (see index)

16 mushrooms, sliced

juice of 1 lemon

¼ teaspoon curry powder

¼ teaspoon cayenne

Preheat oven to 350°F. Season chicken pieces with salt, pepper, and nutmeg; dip in milk, then dip in flour (reserve remaining flour for use later). Melt ½ cup of the butter in a 2-quart, ovenproof casserole or Dutch oven. Sauté chicken until pieces are firm but not browned. Combine onions and garlic, and add to chicken. Cover casserole and bake at 350°F. for 10 minutes. Pour wine over chicken and bake 15 minutes longer. Add cream blended with reserved flour and stir until smooth. Add Chicken Broth. Reduce oven temperature to 300°F. Cover casserole and return it to oven. Bake at 300°F. for 30 minutes. Sauté mushrooms in the remaining

2 tablespoons butter in a skillet, and sprinkle with lemon juice. Cook until liquid is evaporated. Add mushrooms to chicken with the curry and the cayenne. Bake 5 minutes longer. Serves six.

Mustard lends an unusual flavor to squab.

PIGEONNEAU A LA CRAPAUDINE
(BROILED SQUAB CRAPAUDINE)

4 squabs, 1 pound each, split

½ teaspoon each, salt and pepper

1/3 cup vegetable oil

4 tablespoons dry mustard

4 tablespoons white vinegar

1 cup fine, dry bread crumbs

1/3 cup melted butter

3 tablespoons butter

2 lemons cut in half

Preheat broiler. Wash squabs, and pat dry with paper towels. Season squabs, inside and out, with salt and pepper, and brush skin with some of the oil. Place in broiler pan. Broil with broiler pan in middle position for 8 minutes. Turn, brush with oil and broil another 8 minutes. Remove squabs, and cool slightly. Combine mustard and vinegar and with a spatula, spread mixture on all sides of squabs. Dip squabs in bread crumbs to coat evenly, and sprinkle with the 1/3 cup melted butter. Put back in broiler, and broil for 10 minutes on each side. Place squabs on heated platter. In a small saucepan, heat the 3 tablespoons butter until golden brown. Spoon some of the butter over each squab. Serve with lemon halves. Serves four.

A favorite in many European hotels because it is light and not filling.

SUPREME DE POULARDE POJARSKI
(SUPREME OF CHICKEN POJARSKI)

2 chicken breasts, halved, skinned, and boned

1 cup soft, white bread crumbs

2/3 cup milk

8 tablespoons butter

4 tablespoons heavy cream

1 teaspoon each, salt and pepper

½ teaspoon nutmeg

¼ cup flour

½ cup melted butter

Chop chicken meat finely. Soak bread crumbs in milk for a few minutes, then squeeze out excess milk. Combine chicken and bread crumbs. Add 8 tablespoons of unmelted butter, cream, salt, pepper, and nutmeg. Mix well and shape mixture into 4 supremes (roughly their original chicken breast shapes). Dust with flour. Melt the ½ cup butter in a skillet, and sauté supremes over low heat until browned on both sides (about 20 minutes). Remove to a platter. Serves four.

The Virginia ham complements the chicken in an interesting fashion.

LA POITRINE DE POULARDE VIRGINIENNE
(BREAST OF CHICKEN VIRGINIA)

2 whole chicken breasts, halved

½ teaspoon each, salt and pepper

1 teaspoon dried thyme

8 tablespoons soft butter

*8 oblong bread croutons,
buttered and browned in oven*

*8 slices 1-ounce size cooked
Smithfield ham, heated*

8 large mushroom caps, broiled

8 tablespoons Maitre d'Hotel Sauce (see index)

Preheat broiler. Arrange chicken breasts on broiler pan. Sprinkle chicken with salt, pepper, and thyme. Brush with some of the butter. Place broiler pan so chicken is about 6 inches from heat source and broil as range manufacturer directs, about 15 minutes on each side. Baste often with more of the butter. To serve, place a crouton on a plate; top with a piece of heated ham, then a breast of chicken. Garnish with mushrooms and top with Maitre d'Hotel Sauce. Serves four.

A delicate white wine adds body and brings out the flavor in this chicken, which is prepared with an Italian flair.

POULET SAUTE ROMANA
(CHICKEN ROMANA)

2 broiler-fryer chickens, 2½ pounds each, cut up

1 teaspoon each, salt and pepper

1 tablespoon dried oregano leaves

juice of 1 lemon

½ cup all-purpose flour

½ cup vegetable oil

2 onions, peeled, quartered, and separated

2 garlic cloves, peeled, chopped, and crushed

4 green peppers, seeded and cut into sixths

2 bay leaves

1 cup dry white wine

1 cup Chicken Stock (see index)

½ cup tomato purée

4 tomatoes, peeled and quartered

2 tablespoons chopped, fresh parsley

1 tablespoon grated lemon peel

Preheat oven to 375°F. Season chicken pieces with salt, pepper, oregano, and lemon juice. Dip pieces in flour. Heat oil in skillet over medium heat, and sauté chicken pieces until browned on all sides. Transfer chicken to a 2-quart casserole; add onions, garlic, peppers, and bay leaves. Bake uncovered at 375°F. for 5 minutes. Add white wine, Chicken Stock, and tomato purée. Cover casserole and bake at 375°F. for 30 minutes, stirring the contents several times. Add tomatoes and bake 20 minutes longer, stirring several times. Adjust salt and pepper seasoning to taste. Remove chicken pieces to a platter; sprinkle with parsley and grated lemon peel, and serve the sauce separately. Serves four.

VEGETABLES

Some kind of vegetable is usually served as a side dish at most dinners, and vegetables also can be combined with meat in limitless ways for main dishes. Vegetables are even used in desserts (*see* index for German Carrot Cake).

The methods of preparing vegetables are as varied as the vegetables themselves—blanching, baking, sautéing, steaming— and a great variety of sauces, herbs, spices, and wines may be added.

Whenever possible try to buy fresh vegetables. If you live in a large city, they will be available all year; in a smaller town, you may have to buy vegetables in season and may at times have to use frozen vegetables. Whatever you do, don't be afraid to experiment. Vegetables deserve special treatment even when they appear as side dishes.

This dish should be started a day in advance.

CHOUX ROUGES BRAISES
(BRAISED RED CABBAGE)

1 medium-sized head red cabbage

¼ cup dry red wine

2 tablespoons vinegar

3 slices bacon, minced

2 teaspoons peeled, chopped onions

1 garlic clove, peeled, crushed, and chopped

½ teaspoon each, salt and pepper

¼ teaspoon sugar

¼ cup Brown Stock (see index)
or canned bouillon

Trim bruised outside leaves from cabbage and discard them. Cut cabbage into quarters and remove core. Cut each quarter into narrow strips and wash in cold water. Drain well. Place cabbage in a large bowl. Stir in wine and vinegar. Cover and refrigerate overnight. Drain well. Fry bacon in a saucepan until golden; add onions and garlic, and cook until golden brown. Add cabbage, salt, pepper, sugar, and Brown Stock. Bring to a boil. Cover and simmer for 40 minutes. Serves four.

An unusual taste for this vegetable.

CHOUX VERTS BAVARIAN
(BAVARIAN CABBAGE)

1 medium-sized head cabbage

*1 teaspoon salt plus ½ teaspoon each,
salt and pepper*

2 tablespoons butter

¼ cup Béchamel Sauce (see index)

½ cup sour cream

¼ teaspoon nutmeg

Trim bruised outside leaves from cabbage and discard them. Wash, quarter, and remove core. Place cabbage in a 4-quart kettle, and barely cover cabbage with water. Add 1 teaspoon salt. Cook for 20 minutes over medium heat. Drain and rinse under cold running water. Put cabbage in a tea towel and squeeze out water. Chop cabbage coarsely. Melt butter in a 10-inch skillet. Sauté cabbage until heated throughout. Add Béchamel Sauce and sour cream. Bring to a boil. Season with salt, pepper, and nutmeg. Serves four.

Fresh mushrooms are far superior to canned ones, and you should always try to use them in a recipe like this.

CHAMPIGNONS GENEVOISE
(MUSHROOMS IN CREAM)

2 tablespoons butter

1½ pounds mushrooms, washed and sliced

½ teaspoon salt

¼ teaspoon pepper

juice of 1 lemon

1/3 cup dry white wine

1 teaspoon flour

¾ cup heavy cream

¼ teaspoon nutmeg

Melt butter in a 9-inch skillet. Add mushrooms; season with salt, pepper, and lemon juice. Cook over moderately high heat so the water rendered from the mushrooms reduces quickly. When moisture is gone, add wine and cook until liquid is reduced to half volume. Sprinkle flour over mushrooms, mix well. Add cream and let cook until the sauce has thickened slightly. Season with nutmeg. Serves six to eight.

CHAMPIGNONS BORDELAISE
(MUSHROOMS BORDELAISE)

2 tablespoons butter

1½ pounds mushrooms, washed and sliced

½ teaspoon salt

½ teaspoon pepper

juice of 1 lemon

½ cup dry red wine

¾ cup Brown Sauce (see index)

Melt butter in a 9-inch skillet. Add mushrooms, salt, pepper, and lemon juice. Cook over moderately high heat so that the water rendered from the mushrooms reduces quickly. When moisture is gone, add wine and cook until liquid is reduced to half its volume. Add Brown Sauce. Bring to a boil and simmer for 2 minutes. Add more salt and pepper if needed. Serves six to eight.

PETITS POIS A LA FRANCAISE
(GREEN PEAS FRENCH STYLE)

2 teaspoons butter

8 pearl onions, peeled and cut in half

2 cups shelled peas

1 heart of lettuce, shredded

1 teaspoon flour

¼ teaspoon salt

½ teaspoon sugar

¼ cup Chicken Broth (see index) or canned broth

Melt butter in a 2-quart saucepan. Add onions and sauté for 3 minutes. Add peas and lettuce, and sprinkle with flour, salt, and sugar. Mix well. Add Chicken Broth and bring to a boil. Cover and simmer gently for about 35 minutes. Serve very hot. Serves four to six.

PETITS POIS A LA MENTHE
(MINTED PEAS)

2 cups shelled peas

¼ cup water

½ teaspoon salt

½ teaspoon pepper

2 teaspoons chopped, fresh mint leaves

1 tablespoon soft butter

In a saucepan, cook peas in the water, salt, pepper, and mint leaves for 15 minutes. Drain peas and reserve liquid. Put peas in a serving dish and keep warm. Reduce the liquid over high heat to a few tablespoonfuls, and pour this over the peas. Top with butter and serve immediately. Serves four to six.

POIS MANGE-TOUT ETUVES
(SNOW PEAS IN BUTTER)

1 pound snow peas

1/3 cup butter

1 tablespoon peeled, chopped shallots

1 small garlic clove, peeled and chopped

½ teaspoon each, salt and pepper

1 tablespoon flour

¼ cup Chicken Broth (see index) or canned broth

1 tablespoon chopped, fresh parsley

Preheat oven to 375°F. Wash snow peas thoroughly. Melt butter in saucepan with oven-proof handle, and sauté shallots and garlic until golden brown. Add snow peas, salt, pepper, and flour; stir until well mixed. Add Chicken Broth; bring to a boil and remove from heat. Cover pan and bake at 375°F. for 8 minutes. Serve peas in a bowl sprinkled with parsley. Serves four to six.

Chestnuts, rarely seen at most dinner tables, have a high nutritional value. Although not a vegetable, I am still including this delicious recipe in this section as it may be substituted for the vegetable.

MARRONS GLACES AU BEURRE
(GLAZED CHESTNUTS)

1 pound chestnuts, shelled

2 tablespoons butter

1 tablespoon sugar

1 cup White Stock (see index)

2 celery stalks, each cut in half

*1 small bouquet garni (2 sprigs parsley,
1 bay leaf, 1 sprig thyme)*

Soak shelled chestnuts in water at room temperature overnight. Drain chestnuts on paper towel. Preheat oven to 350°F. Melt butter in a 4-quart saucepan with oven-proof handle. Add sugar and cook until brown (caramelized). Quickly add the chestnuts, and stir vigorously until all are coated with the sugar mixture. Add stock, celery, and bouquet garni tied in cheesecloth. Bring to a boil. Cover pan and bake at 350°F. for 40 minutes. When chestnuts are soft, remove pan from oven to top of range and place over medium heat. Discard bouquet garni and celery, and let liquid reduce until chestnuts are coated by the sauce, stirring occasionally. Serves four to six.

Asparagus, which comes into season in mid-summer, is deservedly a popular vegetable.

ASPERGES A LA FONDUE AU GRUYERE
(ASPARAGUS WITH CHEESE FONDUE)

1 pound asparagus

1 cup Cheese Fondue (see index)

6 eggs, shirred (see index)

Wash asparagus spears thoroughly. Peel off any brown spots and little leaves that may hold sand. Place in a 4-quart saucepan with ½ cup water and boil gently for 20 minutes. Drain and put spears on a heated plate and ladle Cheese Fondue, which is very hot, over the points. Top with shirred eggs. Serve hot. Serves six.

Generally, a compote refers to a dish of stewed fruits. A compote is also a serving dish with a pedestal base used for stewed fruits, nuts, and candies. This compote, using Mediterranean vegetables, is a lovely combination of flavors.

COMPOTE D'AUBERGINES ANDALOUSE
(EGGPLANT COMPOTE)

1/3 cup vegetable oil

2 medium-sized eggplants, peeled and cubed

2 onions, peeled and coarsely chopped

2 garlic cloves, peeled, crushed, and chopped

2 tablespoons dried thyme leaves

6 tomatoes, peeled, seeded, and cubed

1 teaspoon salt

½ teaspoon pepper

2 tablespoons chopped, fresh parsley

Heat oil in a 10-inch skillet, and sauté eggplant until lightly browned. Remove with a slotted spoon and keep warm. Add onions and garlic to skillet, and sauté until golden brown. Add eggplant, thyme, and tomatoes. Season with salt and pepper; bring to a boil and cover skillet. Turn off heat and let stand for 30 minutes. Serve garnished with parsley. Serves six.

HARICOTS VERTS MENAGERE
(GREEN BEANS MENAGERE)

½ pound green beans

1/3 cup butter

¼ cup peeled, chopped onions

1 garlic clove, peeled, crushed, and chopped

½ teaspoon salt

¼ teaspoon pepper

fresh chopped parsley

Wash the beans in cold water. Snap off ends and cut each bean in half, crossway on bias. Heat butter in a 10-inch skillet. Add onions and garlic, and sauté until golden brown. Add green beans and season with salt and pepper. Cook, stirring with a spatula, until the butter becomes clear and the beans are crisp (about 10 minutes). Put them in a bowl and garnish with parsley. Serves four.

This is one of the simplest and most delicious ways of preparing green beans.

HARICOTS VERTS AU BEURRE
(BOILED GREEN BEANS IN BUTTER)

1 pound small green beans

1 teaspoon salt

½ cup butter

Wash the beans in cold water and trim ends. Put beans into a 4-quart saucepan and cover with boiling water. Add salt. Boil uncovered for 15 minutes. The beans will remain green and crisp. Drain well. Heat butter in a 9-inch skillet until golden brown. Add beans and sauté for 2 minutes. Serve hot. Serves four.

HARICOTS VERTS BRAISES
(BRAISED GREEN BEANS)

1 pound green beans

1 tablespoon butter

½ onion, peeled and chopped

*1 teaspoon salt for cooking water, plus
½ teaspoon each, salt and pepper*

2 teaspoons flour

1 ham bone with trimmings

*1 small bouquet garni (2 sprigs parsley,
1 sprig thyme, 1 bay leaf tied in cheesecloth)*

1¼ cups White Stock (see index), heated

2 sheets waxed paper

Preheat oven to 350°F. Trim ends off beans and place in a 4-quart saucepan. Cover with boiling water, add 1 teaspoon salt to water and boil for 3 minutes. Drain. Melt butter in an oven-proof casserole. Add onions and sauté until golden brown. Add beans and season with salt, pepper, and flour. Mix well. Place ham bone and bouquet garni in the center of beans. Pour White Stock over beans. Bring to a boil then cover with waxed paper. Cover casserole with a lid. Bake at 350°F. for 1½ hours. Remove from oven, discard bouquet garni and ham bone before serving. Serves four to six.

Potatoes, native to the western hemisphere, were introduced into France in the sixteenth century.

POMMES DE TERRE DAUPHINE
(DAUPHINE POTATOES)

Pâté à chou

½ cup water

pinch of salt

4 tablespoons butter

1 cup sifted all-purpose flour

2 eggs, slightly beaten

Potatoes

6 medium-sized potatoes

½ teaspoon salt

¼ teaspoon pepper

3 tablespoons butter

½ cup hot milk

4 cups lard (2 pounds)

In a bowl, blend all ingredients for pâté à chou until smooth. Set aside. Peel and cut potatoes into medium-sized pieces. Place in a 2-quart saucepan. Cover with water and boil until tender. Drain. Mash potatoes in a large mixing bowl, and blend in pâté à chou. Add salt, pepper, butter, and hot milk; blend thoroughly. Heat lard in a deep 2-quart saucepan over medium-high heat to 375°F. on deep-frying thermometer. Drop potato mixture, a few spoonfuls at a time into the hot fat and brown on all sides. Drain on paper towels and serve hot. Serves six.

POMMES DE TERRE SOUFFLEES
(POTATO SOUFFLE)

4 large potatoes

4 cups lard (2 pounds)

salt to taste

Wash, peel and cut potatoes into thin slices. Pat dry with paper towels. In each of two heavy 2-quart saucepans, place 2 cups of the lard. Heat lard in one pan to 300°F. on a deep-frying thermometer. Heat lard in the other pan to 400°F. on a deep-frying thermometer. Drop a handful of potato slices, one at a time, into the lard at 300°F. Cook until potatoes begin to swell. Stir frequently to prevent slices from sticking together. This will take about 6 to 8 minutes. Scoop out slices and plunge them immediately into the second pan with the lard at 400°F. This causes the slices to puff at once. Turn until brown and crisp. Remove and drain on paper towels. Sprinkle with salt to taste and keep warm. Repeat process until all potatoes are cooked. Serve immediately. Serves four.

GRATIN DAUPHINOIS
(CHEESE POTATOES)

6 medium-sized potatoes

½ teaspoon each, salt and pepper

1 teaspoon dried thyme leaves

1 garlic clove, peeled and chopped

1 tablespoon butter

1½ tablespoons grated Gruyère cheese

1 egg, slightly beaten

¾ cup light cream

Preheat oven to 375°F. Peel and slice potatoes very thin. Sprinkle with salt, pepper, thyme, and garlic; mix well. Butter a shallow 2-quart baking dish, and arrange potatoes in layers, sprinkling cheese on each layer. Mix egg with cream and pour mixture over the potatoes. Bake uncovered at 375°F. for 40 minutes, or until potatoes are tender and top is brown. Serves four.

POMMES DE TERRE DARPHIN
(POTATOES DARPHIN)

6 medium-sized potatoes

¼ cup butter

½ teaspoon each, salt and pepper

½ garlic clove, peeled, crushed, and chopped

Peel and cut potatoes into thin strips. Soak potatoes in a pan of cold water for 20 minutes. Drain well. Melt butter in a 9-inch skillet and add potatoes. Season with salt, pepper, and garlic; mix well. Brown potatoes on one side, then turn with a wide spatula and brown on other side. Simmer until done. Serves four.

POMMES DE TERRE CHAMPS ELYSEES
(POTATOES CHAMPS ELYSEES)

Follow same procedure as for Potato Darphin, but add 1/3 cup julienne-style truffles or morels and 1/3 cup julienne-style mushrooms after potatoes are browned.

OIGNONS GLACES
(GLAZED ONIONS)

1 tablespoon butter

1 pound small pearl onions, peeled

½ teaspoon salt

2 teaspoons sugar

¼ cup Brown Stock (see index)

2 sheets waxed paper

Preheat oven to 350°F. Melt butter in a 9-inch skillet with oven-proof handle. Add onions and sprinkle with salt and sugar. Sauté onions over medium heat until golden brown. Add the Brown Stock, bring to a boil and cover onions with waxed paper. Cover the skillet with a lid. Bake at 350°F. for 20 minutes. Remove skillet from oven and place over direct heat. Simmer until the stock is completely absorbed by the onions. Serves six.

Oyster plant, also referred to as salsify, is a root vegetable. It can be prepared in many ways, and the recipe below is one of the more unusual.

SALSIFIS AUX FINES HERBES PROVENÇALE
(OYSTER PLANT PROVENÇALE)

¼ cup flour

4 cups cold water

juice of 1 lemon

2 teaspoons salt

1 bunch oyster plant, about 3 pounds

2 tablespoons butter

½ teaspoon salt

½ teaspoon pepper

2 tablespoons chopped, fresh parsley

1 garlic clove, peeled and chopped

In a small bowl, mix flour with ½ cup of the cold water to make a smooth paste. Gradually add paste to remaining 3½ cups water in 4-quart saucepan. Add lemon juice and salt, and bring to a boil. Peel or scrape the oyster plant roots. Wash and cut into 2-inch strips; drop immediately into the boiling liquid. Bring to a boil and cook for 10 minutes. As soon as pieces can be easily pierced with a fork, they are done. Do not overcook. Drain in a colander. Heat butter in a 9-inch skillet until it is golden brown. Add the oyster plant; season with salt and pepper, and add parsley mixed with the garlic. Toss until well blended. Serves four to six.

CHOUX DE BRUXELLES AU BEURRE
(BRUSSELS SPROUTS IN BUTTER)

1 quart Brussels sprouts

1/3 cup butter

1/3 cup peeled, chopped onions

½ teaspoon each, salt and pepper

½ teaspoon nutmeg

Wash Brussels sprouts in cold water, and trim off bottoms and any bruised leaves. Put Brussels sprouts in a 2-quart saucepan, and cover with boiling water and ½ teaspoon salt. Cook for 10 minutes. Drain in a colander. Melt butter in a 9-inch skillet and add onions. Sauté until golden brown. Add the cooked Brussels sprouts, and season with salt, pepper, and nutmeg. Mix well; cover and let simmer for 5 minutes over medium heat. Serves six.

CHOUX DE BRUXELLES AUX MARRONS
(BRUSSELS SPROUTS WITH CHESTNUTS)

1 quart Brussels sprouts

1/3 cup butter

2 teaspoons sugar

½ cup cooked, chopped chestnuts

½ teaspoon salt

½ teaspoon pepper

¼ teaspoon nutmeg

*¼ cup Chicken Broth (see index)
or canned chicken broth*

2 sheets waxed paper

Preheat oven to 350°F. Wash Brussels sprouts in cold water, and trim off bottoms and any bruised leaves. Put Brussels sprouts in a 2-quart saucepan, and cover with boiling water and ½ teaspoon salt. Cook for 10 minutes. Drain in a colander. Melt butter in a 9-inch skillet with an oven-proof handle. Add sugar and cook until golden. Add chestnuts to sugar, and sauté for a minute or two. Add Brussels sprouts, salt, pepper, and nutmeg, mix well. Heat broth and pour over Brussels sprouts. Cover with waxed paper and then a lid. Bake at 350°F. for 30 minutes. Serve in covered dish to keep warm. Serves six.

CELERI BRAISE
(BRAISED CELERY)

4 celery hearts

½ teaspoon salt

1 cup Chicken Broth (see index)

1 bay leaf

1 onion, peeled

2 whole cloves

2 tablespoons butter

juice of 1 lemon

2 tablespoons chopped, fresh parsley

Preheat oven to 350°F. Remove outer stalks of celery, reserving them for other use. Wash hearts and put in a saucepan. Cover with boiling water and ½ teaspoon salt. Cook for 3 minutes. Drain hearts and place in a 1-quart saucepan with oven-proof handle. Add Chicken Broth, bay leaf, and onion studded with cloves. Cover and bake at 350°F. for 1 hour. Remove celery hearts to a heated platter, Discard onion and reduce liquid over high heat to half its volume. Add butter, lemon juice, and parsley; pour over celery. Serves four.

Carrots are available year-round. This is one of the simplest—and most delicious ways to prepare them.

CAROTTES GLACEES
(GLAZED CARROTS)

30 small finger-sized carrots

1 cup water

1/3 cup butter

½ teaspoon sugar

½ teaspoon salt

¼ teaspoon pepper

Scrub carrots and place in a 2-quart saucepan. Add water, butter, sugar, salt, and pepper. Bring to a boil. Cook uncovered for 10 to 15 minutes, or until carrots are tender and liquid has evaporated. Carrots will be glazed with butter. Serves six to eight.

CAROTTES VICHY
(VICHY CARROTS)

15 medium-sized carrots

3 tablespoons butter

1 cup carbonated water

½ teaspoon each, salt and pepper

½ teaspoon sugar

2 tablespoons chopped, fresh parsley

Peel or scrape carrots; wash and cut into thin crosswise slices. Place in a 2-quart saucepan. Add butter, carbonated water, salt, pepper, and sugar. Cook uncovered slowly for 20 minutes, until liquid has evaporated and carrots are lightly glazed. Sprinkle with parsley. Serves six to eight.

Cauliflower, native to the Orient, was popular in Italy as early as the sixteenth century.

CHOU-FLEUR AU BEURRE
(CAULIFLOWER IN BUTTER)

1 head cauliflower

1/3 cup butter

½ teaspoon each, salt and pepper

juice of 1 lemon

2 tablespoons parsley

Break flowerets from cauliflower head, and place them in a 4-quart saucepan. Cover with boiling water. Bring to a boil; reduce heat to medium, and cook for 8 to 10 minutes. Drain and dry cauliflower in towel. Heat butter in a 10-inch skillet until golden brown. Put cauliflower flowerets in butter and sauté for 3 minutes, or until lightly browned. Season with salt, pepper, and lemon juice. Put cauliflower in serving bowl and sprinkle with parsley. Serves six.

CHOU-FLEUR MENAGERE
(BOILED CAULIFLOWER MENAGERE)

1 head cauliflower

2 tablespoons butter

2 tablespoons flour

1/3 cup heavy cream

½ teaspoon each, salt and pepper

¼ teaspoon ground nutmeg

juice of 1 lemon

2 tablespoons chopped fresh parsley

Trim away outside green leaves and wash cauliflower well. Place whole head in a saucepan just large enough so cauliflower fits snugly. Half cover with boiling water and 1 teaspoon salt. Cover and simmer 20 to 30 minutes until just fork tender. Remove cauliflower to a heated serving dish and keep warm. Reserve broth. Melt butter in a 4-quart saucepan; add flour and mix well. Add 1 cup of slightly cooled cauliflower broth; mix until smooth, and simmer for 10 minutes. Remove pan from heat and stir in cream. Bring to a boil over low heat. Season with salt, pepper, nutmeg, and lemon juice. Strain sauce over cauliflower. Sprinkle with parsley. Serves six.

Spinach was brought to Europe from Persia by the Moors.

VELOUTE D'EPINARDS
(VELOUTE OF SPINACH)

2 pounds spinach

1 cup boiling water

1/3 cup Béchamel Sauce (see index)

½ teaspoon each, salt and pepper

1 pinch of nutmeg

1/3 cup butter

Remove stems and any bruised leaves from spinach. Wash several times in warm water. Place in a 4-quart saucepan. Add boiling water and cook for 5 minutes. Drain and squeeze out as much water as possible. Rub spinach through a fine sieve or purée in an electric blender. Heat Béchamel Sauce in a 2-quart saucepan; add spinach, salt, pepper, and nutmeg; simmer for 3 minutes. Heat butter until golden brown in a small skillet and mix into spinach. Serves four to six.

COURGETTES FARCIES ORIENTALE
(STUFFED ZUCCHINI ORIENTAL)

Zucchini

3 medium-sized zucchini

1 onion, peeled and sliced

1/3 cup melted butter

½ cup Brown Stock (see index), heated

Stuffing

1 cup lean lamb, ground

1 tablespoon chopped, peeled shallots

½ cup raw rice, cooked until almost done

1 tablespoon chopped, fresh parsley

1 teaspoon dried thyme leaves

1 teaspoon curry powder

2 tablespoons seedless raisins

½ teaspoon each, salt and pepper

Preheat oven to 350°F. Wash and scrub zucchini. Cut off ends. With a small spoon, scoop out inside pulp, leaving a shell about ½ inch thick. Chop and reserve pulp. Mix all ingredients for stuffing and chopped zucchini pulp. Fill zucchini shells with stuffing. Spread sliced onions on the bottom of an 8-inch square pan. Arrange zucchini on onions. Combine butter and Brown Stock, and pour over zucchini. Cover and bake at 350°F. for 30 minutes. Remove cover and continue to bake until all liquid is absorbed. Spoon drippings over zucchini frequently. Serves six.

South American in origin, tomatoes are sometimes called "love apples."

TOMATES CONCASSEES
(STEWED TOMATOES)

8 large tomatoes

1 tablespoon butter

1 large onion, peeled and chopped

4 garlic cloves, peeled, crushed, and chopped

1 teaspoon sugar

½ teaspoon salt

¼ teaspoon pepper

*1 bouquet garni (1 sprig thyme, 2 sprigs parsley,
1 bay leaf tied in cheesecloth)*

Drop tomatoes one at a time into boiling water; remove immediately and plunge into cold water. Slip off skins. Squeeze out seeds and cut pulp into small pieces. Melt butter in a 2-quart saucepan; add onion and garlic. Sauté until golden brown. Add tomatoes, sugar, salt, pepper, and bouquet garni, let simmer until most of the moisture evaporates. Discard bouquet garni. Serves four.

SALADS

When salad is mentioned, too many Americans think of lettuce, and, unfortunately, they also think of an uninspired dish. A salad need not be lettuce—and it need not be uninspired. In no other area of cooking are you as free to experiment with flavors, textures, and colors.

The options in salad making are limited only by your imagination, so don't be afraid to improvise with recipes in this chapter. In fact, I have concluded the chapter with a list of salad combinations frequently used at The Greenbrier. These are intended merely as suggestions, bases upon which to build other combinations of new, exciting salad dishes.

One of the most elegant dishes you can prepare, and possibly the ultimate of salads.

SALADE DE HOMARD
(LOBSTER SALAD)

2 pounds cooked lobster

4 hard-cooked egg whites

½ cup diced celery

1 cup Greenbrier Lorenzo Dressing (see index)

salt and pepper to taste

6 lettuce leaves

2 hard-cooked egg yolks

Remove lobster meat from shell, and slice it into ½-inch pieces. Cut egg whites into medium-sized pieces. Put lobster and egg whites in a bowl with the celery. Add dressing and toss lightly until well mixed; season to taste with salt and pepper. Chill 1 hour. Serve salad on lettuce leaves. Rub egg yolks through a fine sieve, and use to garnish top of salad. Serves six.

Caesar Salad was created in a restaurant in Tijuana, Mexico, during the 20s.

CAESAR SALAD

4 hearts romaine lettuce

2 garlic cloves, peeled and crushed

2 fillets anchovies, mashed

1 teaspoon dry mustard

¼ teaspoon each, salt and pepper

½ cup grated (or crumbled) blue cheese

½ cup olive oil

juice of one lemon

2 dashes Worchestershire sauce

1 dash Tabasco sauce

2 coddled eggs (see index)

½ cup bread croutons

Wash hearts of romaine in cold water; drain and shake dry. Separate leaves and break into small pieces. Place lettuce in wooden bowl that has been rubbed with garlic and anchovies. Sprinkle mustard over the lettuce; add salt, pepper, and cheese. Add oil, lemon juice, Worcestershire and Tabasco sauces. Break coddled eggs over salad and toss gently until well mixed and lettuce has absorbed liquid. Add more salt and pepper, if necessary. When salad is served, add croutons, tossing salad once more. Serves eight.

A light and tasty salad that is perfect for brunch or lunch.

SALADE DE VOLAILLE
(CHICKEN SALAD)

2 cups cubed, cooked chicken

1 cup diced celery

6 hard-cooked egg whites, coarsely chopped

juice of one lemon

¼ teaspoon each, salt and pepper

1 cup mayonnaise (see index)

½ cup sour cream

6 lettuce leaves

1 tablespoon drained capers

2 teaspoons paprika

In a bowl, combine chicken, celery, egg whites, and lemon juice. Add salt and pepper. Mix mayonnaise and sour cream together, and fold into the chicken mixture. Cover and let stand for 1 hour in refrigerator. Arrange salad on lettuce leaves; top with capers and sprinkle with paprika. Serves six.

A change of pace from the traditional lettuce and dressing salads.

SALADE DE CHAMPIGNONS
(MUSHROOM SALAD)

1 pound fresh, white mushrooms

juice of 2 lemons

¼ teaspoon each, salt and pepper

3 tablespoons vegetable oil

2 tablespoons chopped parsley

1 garlic clove, peeled, crushed, and chopped

Wash and dry mushrooms, and cut into thin slices. Put mushrooms in a bowl; drizzle with lemon juice, and season with salt and pepper. Add oil and toss lightly. Sprinkle with chopped parsley and garlic. Serves four.

A hearty and robust salad that will perk up a menu.

GERMAN POTATO SALAD

12 medium-sized potatoes

¼ teaspoon each, salt and pepper

6 slices bacon

1½ cups peeled, chopped onions

2 garlic cloves, crushed and chopped

¼ cup prepared mustard

½ cup dry white wine

½ cup white wine vinegar

1 cup Chicken Broth (see index)

1 cup vegetable oil

½ cup chopped, fresh parsley

Wash and cook potatoes in skins in boiling, salted water until tender. Cool 20 minutes. Peel and cut potatoes in thin slices. Put in a bowl, and add salt and pepper. Cut bacon very fine, and sauté in a saucepan over moderate heat. When fat has rendered, add onions and garlic and sauté until golden brown. Add mustard, wine, vinegar, and Chicken Broth; bring to a boil. Add oil and remove from heat. Gently mix hot dressing into potatoes and add parsley. Serve lukewarm. Serves eight.

One of the truly exquisite salads of the world. This is a wonderful summer luncheon.

SALADE NIÇOISE

6 small artichoke hearts, cooked

2 cups cooked, sliced green beans

1 ripe avocado, peeled and cubed

13 ounces tuna, drained (2 cans, 6½ ounce size)

1 cup pitted, black olives

4 medium-sized potatoes, boiled, peeled, and diced

1½ cups Basic French Dressing (see index)

6 lettuce leaves

6 ripe tomatoes, peeled and quartered

6 hard-cooked eggs, halved

12 anchovy fillets

6 sprigs fresh parsley

salt and pepper to taste

Put artichokes, green beans, avocado, tuna, olives, potatoes, and Basic French Dressing in a bowl, and toss lightly. Cover and chill 2 to 3 hours. To serve, put mixture on lettuce leaves arranged on individual dinner plates. Garnish with tomatoes, eggs, anchovies, and parsley. Sprinkle with salt and pepper to taste. Serves six.

SALADS SERVED AT THE GREENBRIER

AIDA

Sliced grapefruit and pineapple in alternate layers on lettuce hearts, garnished with walnuts, French dressing.

AIGLON

Shredded lettuce, tomatoes, French-style green beans, and truffles cut into julienne; dress with light cream and mayonnaise with anchovy sauce.

ALBERTINE

Romaine, sliced avocado, sliced orange, skinned and pitted grapes.

ALEXANDRA

Peach half, julienne of celery and grapefruit in slices, sliced red peppers, chopped nuts, and mayonnaise.

ALICE

Romaine, slices of grapefruit and orange, chopped green peppers, and walnuts; French dressing.

ALMA

Romaine with slices of orange and grapefruit, garnished with sliced, ripe olives and crossed red and green peppers.

ANNA

Leaves from hearts of lettuce, sliced tomatoes, celery, and apples cut into julienne.

AUGUSTINE

Lettuce, sliced avocado, grapes.

ANTOINETTE

Lettuce, sliced pineapple, cream cheese; red pepper as garnish.

ARGENTEUIL

Lettuce, cooked asparagus tips, red peppers.

BEATRICE

Lettuce filled with cooked green beans in center, bordered by sliced beets, topped with French dressing.

BELVEDERE

Chicory and escarole topped with sliced apples and beets; dressed with mayonnaise mixed to taste with chili sauce.

BON TON

Heart of lettuce topped by cooked asparagus tips, sliced tomato, Basic French Dressing.

CAPRICE

Slice of pineapple on lettuce leaf, quartered tomato on top, and mayonnaise dressing.

CASINO

Avocado, grapefruit, and orange served on chicory, garnished with red and green pepper, Basic French Dressing.

CHATELAINE

Romaine and watercress, cooked asparagus tips, and sliced beets.

CORDON ROUGE

Lettuce, sliced celery knobs, a border of diced beets.

DIPLOMATE

Lettuce base; pineapple, apples, and julienne celery; chopped walnuts as garnish. Mayonnaise dressing.

DOCTOR

Lettuce topped with tomatoes and cottage cheese; watercress as garnish.

DOROTHY

Romaine topped with slices of orange, grapefruit, and avocado; garnished with red pepper.

DUCHESSES

Lettuce, cooked asparagus tips, slices of apple, celery cut in julienne; finely chopped truffles as garnish.

EMILY

Romaine, cooked asparagus tips, grapefruit, strips of red and green peppers.

FAVORITE

Lettuce, slices of avocado, diced celery, pimiento, ripe olives.

GAULOISE

Romaine, cooked asparagus tips, celery, mushrooms, truffles, all in julienne, tossed; Basic French Dressing.

GENEVA

Romaine, sliced hard-cooked eggs, sliced beets.

GOURMAND

Lettuce, sliced orange, apples, and pears; mayonnaise dressing.

HAWLEY

Endive, watercress, sliced mushrooms; Basic French Dressing.

JONA

Fresh apricot halves on lettuce filled with cottage cheese, garnished with watercress.

LOUISE

Heart of lettuce, julienne of cooked chicken and ham.

MATHILDE

Romaine, sliced avocado, apples and cucumbers, chopped walnuts.

MIAMI

Grapefruit and orange sections on romaine.

MERRY WIDOW

Romaine, alternate slices of avocado, and strips of red and green peppers; Basic French Dressing.

TOMATO LILY

Tomato cut back to resemble lily and topped with chopped cucumbers in mayonnaise.

TOSCA

Romaine, celery, green beans, sliced tomatoes; Basic French Dressing.

WALDORF

Lettuce, apples, celery, mayonnaise, and nuts with sour cream topping.

SALAD DRESSINGS

The art of selecting the proper salad dressing to complement a salad is something you learn through experimentation. The best way to begin is to combine dressings and salad ingredients that have appeal for you. Salad dressing is often the fillip that makes a salad memorable.

Generally, vinaigrette and its many variations are used on green salads. Heartier dressings, often with a mayonnaise base, are used in meat and seafood salads. There is no set rule, however, and you may find a vinegar-and-oil combination that is perfect on a meat salad—you may even want to create your own salad dressings.

In the following pages, I am sharing with you the very finest—and most popular—dressings that we serve at The Greenbrier. Their uses are endless.

Bottled French dressing is far different from the classic oil and vinegar dressings of French cookery. Here is a basic French dressing, plus a number of variations on this splendid original theme. This recipe can be cut proportionately into smaller portions.

VINAIGRETTE FRANÇAISE
(BASIC FRENCH DRESSING)

1 tablespoon dry mustard

1 cup red or white wine vinegar

3 cups vegetable oil

1 teaspoon each, salt and pepper

1 teaspoon sugar

In a bowl mix mustard and vinegar thoroughly. Beat in oil. Season with salt and pepper. Add sugar to taste, if vinegar is too sour. Yields 1 quart.

VARIATIONS

VINAIGRETTE ITALIENNE

(Italian Dressing)

1 garlic clove, peeled

1 tablespoon finely chopped, fresh parsley

1 tablespoon tomato purée

1 cup Basic French Dressing

salt and pepper to taste

Crush and chop garlic and mix with parsley in a bowl. Add tomato purée and mix well. Fold in Basic French Dressing, and add salt and pepper to taste. Yields 1 cup.

VINAIGRETTE AUX ANCHOIS

(Anchovy Dressing)

½ cup anchovy fillets

1/3 cup grated, peeled onion

1 tablespoon chopped, fresh parsley

2 cups Basic French Dressing

Blend anchovies with onions and parsley in an electric blender until smooth. Add to Basic French Dressing.

VINAIGRETTE ESPAGNOLE

(Spanish Dressing)

1 garlic clove, peeled

1 teaspoon diced, canned pimiento

1 teaspoon dry mustard

1 teaspoon chili powder

1 cup Basic French Dressing

salt and pepper to taste

Crush and chop garlic and mix well with pimientos, dry mustard, and chili powder in a bowl. Fold in Basic French Dressing, and add salt and pepper to taste. Yields 1 cup.

VINAIGRETTE A LA GREENBRIER
(GREENBRIER VINAIGRETTE)

3 cups vegetable oil

1 cup white wine vinegar

½ teaspoon salt

¼ teaspoon pepper

1 cup peeled, chopped onions

1 cup peeled, diced tomatoes

½ cup diced, hard-cooked egg whites

½ cup chopped, fresh parsley

2 garlic cloves, peeled, crushed, and chopped

In a bowl, beat oil and vinegar together. Season with salt and pepper, and add all other ingredients. Mix well and serve. Do not keep this dressing longer than two days because onions become flat and alter the taste. Yields 6 cups.

SAUCE ROQUEFORT A LA GREENBRIER
(GREENBRIER ROQUEFORT CHEESE DRESSING)

3 eggs, well beaten

1 tablespoon dry mustard

1 garlic clove, peeled, crushed, and chopped

¼ teaspoon each, salt and pepper

4 cups vegetable oil

1 cup white wine vinegar

juice of one lemon

1 tablespoon A-1 Sauce

1 tablespoon Worcestershire sauce

½ teaspoon Tabasco sauce

1 cup crumbled Roquefort cheese

In a bowl, mix eggs with mustard, garlic, salt, and pepper. Slowly add oil, whipping constantly with a wire whip. When thick, add vinegar, lemon, A-1 Sauce, Worcestershire and Tabasco sauces, and mix well. Fold in Roquefort cheese and serve at once. Yields 6 cups.

SAUCE LORENZO A LA GREENBRIER
(GREENBRIER LORENZO DRESSING)

3 eggs

1 tablespoon dry mustard

1 tablespoon sugar

¼ teaspoon each, salt and pepper

4 cups vegetable oil

1 cup white wine vinegar

1 tablespoon minced, peeled garlic

juice of one lemon

1 tablespoon A-1 sauce

2 tablespoons Worcestershire sauce

½ teaspoon Tabasco sauce

1 tablespoon chili powder

1 cup chopped watercress

½ cup chopped, fresh parsley

In a bowl, beat eggs with mustard, sugar, salt, and pepper. Slowly add oil, whipping constantly with a wire whip. When thick, add vinegar, garlic, lemon, A-1 Sauce, Worcestershire and Tabasco sauces, and chili powder; mix well. Fold in watercress and parsley. Yields 6 cups.

PASTRY AND BAKERY

I have combined these two categories because they share a common ingredient: flour. At The Greenbrier, we have a bakery and a pastry room. Each is equipped with ovens, working counters, and storage racks for the finished products. There is a common section between the two rooms that is equipped with beaters and blenders to whip and blend to the finest possible consistency puddings, pie fillings, meringues, pastry creams, dessert soufflés, and icings.

The pastry-bakery operation is an important one because any meal is only as good as its bakery selection. In addition, dessert should be the grand finale to a good meal—another reason why it should be outstanding.

CREPES SUZETTE

Crêpe Batter

3 eggs

2 tablespoons sugar

½ cup sifted flour

½ cup milk

1 tablespoon grated orange peel

4 tablespoons Curaçao

3 tablespoons melted butter

1 pinch salt

Sauce

6 tablespoons soft butter

6 tablespoons granulated sugar

1 tablespoon grated orange peel

1 tablespoon grated lemon peel

½ cup orange juice, freshly squeezed

2 tablespoons Curaçao

2 tablespoons Grand Marnier

2 tablespoons cognac

Beat eggs with sugar until frothy. Add flour and milk, and beat vigorously with a wire whip until smooth. Add orange peel, Curaçao, butter, and salt; blend well. Heat a 6-inch crêpe pan or heavy skillet until a few drops of water sprinkled on it sizzle and bounce around. For each crêpe, brush the pan very lightly with oil. Add a little less than 2 tablespoons of batter. Quickly rotate pan to spread batter completely over bottom of pan. Cook about 40 seconds, until top is dry and bottom is lightly browned. Turn and cook second side about 20 seconds. Turn crêpe on a wire rack or napkin. Repeat with remaining batter. Makes 18 pancakes. Brush crêpe pan with butter. Add 4 tablespoons of sugar, and let cook momentarily until lightly browned. Add butter and cook until melted. Add orange juice and peels and sprinkle with Curaçao. Add one crêpe at a time, turn quickly. Fold into quarters, and arrange consecutively in the crêpe pan. Repeat with the remaining crêpes. When finished, sprinkle crêpes with remaining 2 tablespoons sugar, and pour Grand Marnier and cognac over them. Let crêpes simmer for 30 seconds. Flame and serve. Serves six.

GENOISE SPONGE CAKE

6 eggs

1 cup sugar

1 teaspoon vanilla

1 grated peel of lemon

¾ cup all-purpose flour

½ cup cake flour

¼ cup melted butter

Preheat oven to 325°F. Put eggs, sugar, vanilla, and grated lemon peel into a bowl of electric mixer. Heat in a hot water bath and mix constantly with a spoon or mixer until batter reaches a warm temperature. Whip at high speed with an electric mixer until mixture is fluffy and thick. Sift the all-purpose flour and cake flour, and fold into the mixture, followed by the melted butter. Pour into 10-inch cake pan and bake at 325°F. for 30 minutes, or until top springs back when lightly touched with the finger. Turn out of pan onto wire rack to cool.

CHOCOLATE GENOISE

6 eggs

1 cup sugar

1½ teaspoons vanilla

¾ cup cake flour

3 tablespoons unsweetened cocoa

¼ cup melted butter

Preheat oven to 325°F. Put the eggs, sugar, and vanilla in the bowl of an electric mixer. Place in a hot water bath, and, mixing constantly, heat to warm temperature. Then use an electric mixer to whip at high speed until mixture is fluffy and thick. Sift the cake flour and cocoa, and fold into mixture followed by the melted butter. Pour into 10-inch cake pan and bake at 325°F. for 30 minutes, or until top springs back when lightly touched with the finger. Turn out of pan onto wire rack to cool.

CHOCOLATE CREAM PIE

2 tablespoons cornstarch

2 cups milk

1½ tablespoons vanilla extract

1 teaspoon salt

2 egg yolks

2 whole eggs

2 squares bitter chocolate

¼ cup butter

2/3 cup sugar, plus 2 tablespoons

2 egg whites

1 cup heavy cream, whipped

Prepare pie shell and bake. In a mixing bowl, put the cornstarch, ½ cup milk, vanilla, and salt. Mix well; add the yolks and whole eggs, and mix again. Melt the chocolate squares and butter in a saucepan. When melted, add 2/3 cup sugar and mix. Pour in 1½ cups milk and bring to a boil, stirring constantly. Add some of the hot milk to the egg mixture, then strain this into the boiling milk, mixing constantly, until thick. Remove from heat. Make a meringue with the egg whites and 2 tablespoons sugar. Fold this into the cooked filling. Pour into a 9-inch, prebaked pie shell. Let cool. After pie is cold, cover with whipped cream.

CHEESE CAKE

3 pounds cream cheese

¾ cup sugar

½ teaspoon salt

6 eggs

2 tablespoons lemon juice

1¼ teaspoons vanilla extract

*enough finely crushed graham cracker crumbs
to make a thin crust*

Preheat oven to 400°F. Have cream cheese at room temperature before mixing. Put cream cheese, salt, and sugar in large bowl of electric mixer. Mix at medium speed. Slowly add eggs, lemon juice, and vanilla while mixing at medium speed until batter is smooth. Grease a 10-inch pan with 3-inch-high sides. Then dust with graham cracker crumbs. Sprinkle extra crumbs on bottom of pan, and press down to make crust. Pour in mixture and bake at 400°F. from 30 to 35 minutes. Let cool in pan for a few hours. Turn out of pan onto a plate. Place another plate on top, and carefully hold both plates, while you turn them over so the cheese cake is upright. Cut the cake with a wet knife.

POUND CAKE

3½ cups sifted cake flour

1½ teaspoons baking powder

1½ cups butter

½ cup shortening

¾ cup milk

3 cups powdered sugar

5 eggs

2 teaspoons vanilla extract

1½ teaspoons rum extract

Preheat oven to 350°F. Have all ingredients at room temperature. In a large bowl of an electric mixer, add flour, baking powder, butter, and shortening. Combine at slow speed; increase to medium speed, and mix for 4 minutes. Add powdered sugar to milk, then slowly add to the other ingredients, and beat at medium speed for 4 minutes. Slowly add eggs, vanilla, and rum and mix for 4 minutes. Divide batter into two lightly greased and floured loaf pans (12 x 3½ x 2½). Bake at 350°F. for 15 minutes. Then reduce to 325°F., and bake 40 minutes longer, or until top springs back when lightly touched with the finger. Cool in pans, then turn out on rack. Yields 2 loaves.

GERMAN CARROT CAKE

4 cups almond flour

1¼ cups filbert flour

5 cups grated carrots (peeled)

½ cup cornstarch

1 teaspoon cinnamon

½ teaspoon salt

1 grated lemon peel

11 egg yolks

1 1/3 cups sugar

11 egg whites

1 1/3 cups sugar

¾ cup granulated or sliced almonds

Preheat oven to 300°F. Put the almond and filbert flours, carrots, cornstarch, cinnamon, salt, and grated lemon peel into a large mixing bowl. Then set aside. In a small mixing bowl, whip yolks and sugar at high speed. Then mix into the dry ingredients. Beat egg whites and sugar until thick but not stiff. Then fold into base batter. Pour into two 10-inch pans that have been greased heavily and coated with granulated or sliced almonds. Bake at 300°F. for about 1 hour.

This icing is the delicious topping found on German Chocolate Cake.

PECAN COCONUT ICING

4½ cups evaporated milk

1/3 cup butter

11 egg yolks

2½ cups sugar

3¾ cups pecan pieces

5 cups coconut

1 tablespoon vanilla extract

Place all ingredients in a 4-quart saucepan and, stirring constantly, cook over medium heat until thick. Watch carefully that icing does not stick or burn. Let cool for 15 to 20 minutes. Icing should be put on cake while it is hot. Yields 2½ to 3 quarts.

GERMAN CHOCOLATE CAKE

½ cup water

¼ cup milk chocolate, melted

¼ cup bitter chocolate, melted

3 teaspoons vanilla extract

1 teaspoon salt

1 cup sugar

½ cup butter

½ cup shortening

6 egg yolks (approximately ½ cup)

2 cups cake flour, sifted

4½ teaspoons baking soda

1 cup buttermilk

4 egg whites (approximately ½ cup)

½ cup sugar

Preheat oven to 325°F. Mix water, milk chocolate, bitter choco-late, vanilla, and salt; heat to warm temperature. Set aside. Put butter, shortening and sugar in a large bowl of an electric mixer, and cream well. Add yolks and mix. Then add the sifted cake flour and baking soda alternately with the buttermilk and chocolate mixture, and mix until all ingredients are blended. In a separate bowl, beat together the egg whites and sugar. Fold this meringue mixture into the batter with a rubber spatula. Grease two 10-inch round cake pans and dust with flour. Divide batter and pour into the pans. Bake at 325°F. for 40 to 50 minutes. Let cool. Cut each cake in half and fill it with Pecan Coconut Icing (see index). Then apply layer to top of cake and frost cake with icing. Cake can be made into two 2-layer cakes or one large 4-layer cake.

BUTTERCREAM ICING

2 cups butter

1 cup shortening

4½ cups confectioners' sugar

6 egg whites

2 teaspoons vanilla extract

Have butter and shortening at room temperature. Put in a bowl of an electric mixer, and beat until light and fluffy. Add confectioners' sugar and beat for 4 to 5 minutes, then add egg whites and vanilla. Beat again for another 4 to 5 minutes.

CHOCOLATE BUTTERCREAM ICING

Using Buttercream Icing recipe, add 2 tablespoons of melted bittersweet chocolate for every cup of Buttercream Icing.

RICH CHOCOLATE BROWNIES

3 cups sugar

8 eggs

2 tablespoons vanilla extract

¾ cup melted milk chocolate

¾ cup melted bittersweet chocolate

1½ cups cake flour, sifted

1 cup melted butter

1½ cups nuts (walnuts or pecans)

Preheat oven to 350°F. In the large bowl of an electric mixer, combine sugar, eggs, and vanilla and beat at high speed for 10 to 15 minutes. Using a spoon, fold in the chocolate, cake flour, butter, and nuts. Pour into a greased and floured pan approximately 15½ x 10½ x 1½ inches and bake for 25 to 35 minutes at 350°F. Let cool in pan, then turn out and cover with your favorite fudge icing (optional). Yields about seventy 1½ inch squares.

CHOCOLATE FUDGE ICING

½ cup butter

2 tablespoons shortening

½ cup water plus ¼ cup water

4 cups confectioners' sugar

1 teaspoon vanilla extract

6 squares 1-ounce size unsweetened chocolate, melted

In a 1-quart saucepan, combine butter, shortening, and ½ cup of the water. Place over medium heat and stir until butter is melted. Remove from heat. Add sugar and beat until smooth. Add the ¼ cup water, vanilla, and melted chocolate. Beat until smooth and creamy. Yields enough icing for 9-inch, 2-layer cake.

LEMON MERINGUE PIE

1 pastry shell 9-inch size, baked and cooled

2 cups water

grated peel of 1 lemon

1 cup sugar

½ cup cornstarch

4 egg yolks, slightly beaten

juice of 3 lemons

2 tablespoons melted butter

½ teaspoon salt

Classic Meringue (see index)

Prepare pastry shell. In a 2-quart saucepan, bring water to a boil, and add lemon peel and sugar. Mix together cornstarch, egg yolks, and lemon juice. Stir a little of the boiling water into the egg mixture, and add this mixture to rest of boiling water. Cook stirring constantly, until thick. Add melted butter and salt. Pour into the baked pastry shell and cool. When cooled, top with Classic Meringue. Preheat oven to 450°F. Bake 5 to 8 minutes or until golden brown. Cool before serving. Makes 1 pie.

CLASSIC MERINGUE

4 egg whites, at room temperature

⅛ teaspoon cream of tartar

8 tablespoons sugar

vanilla extract to taste

In the large bowl of an electric mixer, beat egg whites and cream of tartar until soft peaks form. Gradually add sugar and beat until stiff peaks form. Fold in vanilla extract to taste. Spread over top of pie or over Baked Alaska bringing to edge of crust and bake 5 to 8 minutes at 450°F.

CHOCOLATE SOUFFLE PUDDING

½ cup butter, soft

½ cup all-purpose flour

2 cups milk, heated

1 tablespoon vanilla extract

5 egg yolks

*1 square unsweetened chocolate,
1-ounce size, melted*

5 egg whites, at room temperature

½ cup sugar

Sabayon or Deluxe Vanilla Sauce (see index)

Mix butter and flour together in mixer to form a lumpy mixture. Set aside. Bring milk and vanilla extract to boil. Add butter and flour mixture to boiling milk, and stir over low heat until smooth and stiff. Remove from heat; pour into mixer bowl, and beat at low speed for 8 to 10 minutes. Add egg yolks, one at a time, and then add melted chocolate. In another mixer bowl, beat egg whites until soft peaks form. Gradually add sugar and beat until stiff peaks form. Fold egg whites into chocolate mixture. Pour mixture into a buttered and sugared 2-quart bowl or mold. Set mold in pan of hot water. Bake at 350°F. for 30 to 40 minutes until soufflé is puffed and level across the top. Serve immediately with Sabayon or Deluxe Vanilla Sauce. Serves eight.

GRAND MARNIER SOUFFLE

½ cup soft butter

½ cup all-purpose flour

2 cups milk

grated peel of 2 oranges

5 egg yolks

½ cup Grand Marnier

5 egg whites

2/3 cup sugar

½ cup macaroons (see index), coarsely crumbled

½ cup Curaçao

Sabayon Sauce (see index)

Preheat oven to 350°F. In a small mixer bowl, mix soft butter and flour until blended. (Mixture may be lumpy.) Set aside. In a two-quart saucepan, bring milk to a boil. Add orange peel and flour mixture, and stir over low heat until smooth and stiff. Remove from heat; pour into mixer bowl, and beat 8 to 10 minutes. Add egg yolks, one at a time, and beat until well blended. Stir in Grand Marnier.

In large mixer bowl, beat egg whites until soft peaks form. Gradually add sugar, and beat until stiff peaks form. Fold egg whites into egg yolk mixture. Pour half of mixture into a 1-quart soufflé dish or mold that has been well buttered and dusted with sugar. Sprinkle crumbled macaroons with Curaçao; arrange macaroons on soufflé mixture, and pour remaining mixture on top of macaroons, filling dish to within ½ inch of top. Set dish in a pan of hot water. Bake at 350°F. for 30 to 40 minutes, or until puffed and level across the top. Serve immediately with Sabayon Sauce. Serves eight.

The pastry cream is an excellent filling for éclairs, cakes, and Boston cream pie.

PASTRY CREAM

1/3 cup cornstarch

1½ cups milk

5 eggs

1 tablespoon vanilla extract

½ teaspoon salt

1 cup sugar

In a mixing bowl, put the cornstarch and ¼ cup of milk and mix well. Then add the eggs, vanilla, and salt, beating until blended. Heat the remaining 1¼ cups milk and sugar in a 2-quart saucepan until bubbles appear around edge of pan. Add some of the hot milk to the eggs to warm; strain into the boiling milk, stirring constantly, and cook until thick. Pour into a bowl; cover with waxed paper and let cool. Yields 1 quart.

This unusual filling is used for tarts and petit fours.

FRANGIPANE

2¼ cups almond paste

1½ cups sugar

10 medium-sized eggs, slightly beaten

¾ cup butter

¾ cup shortening

grated peel of 1 lemon

½ cup sifted all-purpose flour

In a bowl, beat almond paste and sugar together until smooth. Add eggs, a little at a time, blending well after each addition. In a bowl, mix butter and shortening together until smooth. Add grated lemon peel and mix well. Add to almond paste mixture, and combine thoroughly. Stir in flour. Store in refrigerator until ready to use.

DUTCH ALMOND TART

1 jar apricot jam

Frangipane filling (see index)

1 cup confectioners' sugar

2 teaspoons orange extract

2 tablespoons water

Make 9-inch pie shell, saving enough dough for topping. Cover bottom of shell with thin layer of apricot jam. Fill a pastry bag with Frangipane (see index) and force out on top of jam, filling to within ⅛-inch from top. Roll out a piece of pie dough ⅛-inch thick, and cut long strips about ½ inch wide. Place strips in a crisscross design on top of pie. Bake for one hour at 325°F. Heat 3 tablespoons apricot jam, and spread over top of cooked tart. Mix 1 cup confectioners' sugar, 2 teaspoons orange extract, 2 tablespoons water and brush this over top of tart.

MACAROONS

2¼ cups almond paste

1½ cups sugar

¾ cup sifted all-purpose flour

1 cup confectioners' sugar

grated peel of 1 lemon

1 cup egg whites

Preheat oven to 350°F. In a large bowl of an electric mixer, thoroughly mix the almond paste, sugar, flour, confectioners' sugar, and lemon peel. Gradually add egg whites mixing until well blended. Grease cookie sheets and dust lightly with flour. Drop mixture by teaspoonfuls about 1 inch apart onto a cookie sheet. (Mixture may also be forced through a pastry bag.) With a folded damp cloth, hit the top of the macaroons to get rid of the peaks and sprinkle lightly with sugar. Bake at 350°F. for 10 to 12 minutes or until light brown. Cool and remove from pan with spatula. Yields about 150 macaroons.

MARSHMALLOW ICING

6 egg whites

2 cups sugar

1 teaspoon vanilla extract

¼ teaspoon cream of tartar

Put all ingredients in a double boiler (do not let water boil, and be sure water does not touch bottom of top pan), and heat to a hot temperature stirring constantly. Pour this mixture into a large bowl of an electric mixer, and beat until stiff. Yields 1 quart.

DELUXE VANILLA SAUCE

2 cups heavy cream

½ cup sugar

4 egg yolks

1 tablespoon flour

1 tablespoon vanilla extract

¼ teaspoon salt

2 scoops vanilla ice cream

Bring cream and sugar just to a boil in a 2-quart saucepan. Remove from heat. Beat egg yolks, flour, vanilla extract, and salt, and stir in a little of the hot cream-sugar mixture. Add the mixture to the rest of the hot cream. Cook this, stirring constantly (do not over cook), until just thickened. Remove from heat and add ice cream, stirring until melted. This sauce can be served either hot or cold. Yields 1 quart.

BISCUITS

2 cups sifted all-purpose flour

3 teaspoons baking powder

½ teaspoon salt

¼ cup shortening

¾ cup milk

Preheat oven to 450°F. Sift flour, baking powder, and salt into a 2-quart bowl. Add shortening and, with a pastry blender or 2 knives, blend until mixture looks like coarse cornmeal. Make a well in center of mixture. Add milk all at once and mix lightly with a fork until a soft dough is formed. Turn dough out on floured board and knead gently 6 to 8 times. Roll out to a thickness of ½ inch. Cut in 2-inch rounds with a floured biscuit cutter or glass. Place on ungreased cookie sheet about 1 inch apart. Bake at 450°F. for 10 to 12 minutes. Yields 15 biscuits.

This American bread will complement almost any dish, and can be served at breakfast, lunch or dinner.

CORN BREAD

¾ cup all-purpose flour

1½ cups yellow cornmeal

4 teaspoons baking powder

¾ teaspoon salt

1 tablespoon sugar

2 eggs, slightly beaten

1¼ cups milk

¼ cup butter, melted

Preheat oven to 400°F. Sift together dry ingredients. In a medium bowl, combine eggs and milk, Add dry ingredients and blend well, stirring in butter. Pour into well-buttered, 8-inch-square pan or 12 muffin cups. Bake at 400°F. for 30 minutes. Serves six.

HARD ROLLS

½-ounce compressed yeast

1 tablespoon salt

1 tablespoon sugar

1 cup water

1 tablespoon shortening

1 tablespoon diamalt

4 cups sifted all-purpose flour

¼ cup cornmeal, approximately

Place all ingredients in a large bowl and mix for 5 minutes. Place dough in well-greased bowl. Cover and let rise in a warm place (85°F.) for 1½ hours. Fold over several times; cover and let raise 30 minutes. Cut dough into 12 equal portions. Roll each into a cylinder. Place on greased cookie sheet that has been sprinkled with cornmeal. Cover and let rise until double in size. Preheat oven to 400°F. Bake rolls 20 minutes until light brown. Yields 24 rolls.

BRIOCHE
(BREAKFAST ROLLS)

2 eggs

5 tablespoons melted butter

2 tablespoons sugar

½ teaspoon salt

1 cake, 1-ounce-size, yeast

½ cup lukewarm water (105 to 115°F.)

3 cups sifted all-purpose flour

*1 whole egg, slightly beaten and diluted
with 4 tablespoons milk*

Combine 2 eggs, butter, sugar, and salt in a small mixing bowl and blend thoroughly. Mix yeast with water and add to egg mixture. Add flour and knead until smooth. Refrigerate for 1 hour. Divide into small pieces, and place into well greased, standard-sized muffin tins. The dough should only half fill the container. Put small ball of dough on top of each. Cover and let rise in warm place until doubled in size. Preheat oven to 350°F. Brush with the egg and milk mixture, and bake for 15 minutes until brown. Yields twelve to sixteen rolls.

POPOVERS

1 cup sifted all-purpose flour

¼ teaspoon salt

1 cup milk

2 eggs, well beaten

Preheat oven to 400°F. Grease muffin tins or 6 to 8 deep custard cups with lard. Sift together flour and salt in a bowl. Combine milk and eggs and mix well. Add to dry ingredients and beat with a rotary beater until smooth. Fill muffin tins or custard cups half full. Bake at 400°F. for 15 minutes. Then reduce oven temperature to 350°F. With oven door slightly open, bake 15 to 20 minutes longer or until brown. Makes six to eight popovers. Serve at once.

SPOON BREAD

2½ cups milk

1 cup yellow cornmeal

1 teaspoon salt

1½ tablespoons melted butter

4 eggs, separated

1 teaspoon baking powder

Preheat oven to 375°F. Scald 2 cups of the milk in a saucepan. Combine cornmeal and the remaining ½ cup milk. Stir into scalded milk. Add salt and cook over low heat, stirring constantly, until batter reaches the consistency of mush. Remove from heat and stir in melted butter. Cool slightly. Separate eggs. Beat yolks slightly with baking powder, and add to cornmeal mixture. Beat egg whites until stiff but not dry. Fold into cornmeal mixture. Grease an 8-inch-square pan, and pour batter into pan. Bake at 375°F. for 35 minutes until firm. Serves six to eight.

FLAMBES

A flaming dessert is for a very special occasion. For one thing, a flambé takes a lot of time to prepare. A hurried flambé is almost certain not to be a success. In fact, at The Greenbrier flambés are usually prepared in advance, a method that you may wish to follow. At the proper moment, you can add the finishing touches to flambé the dessert, bring it to the table gloriously aflame, and await the compliments that are sure to follow.

As you use the recipes in this chapter, be sure to follow the instructions exactly. Don't substitute ingredients in a flambé or your glorious finale may be a disaster.

A heavy meal calls for a light flambé, and a light dinner gives you an excuse to serve an elegant flambé to your guests.

This special dessert consists of vanilla ice cream, heaped in a ring of a fluffy baba, and topped with a combination of brandied fruits and liqueur that has been flambéed.

FROZEN FLAME CONTINENTAL

Babas

1 cup sifted all-purpose flour

1 package active dry yeast

¼ cup warm water (105° to 115°F.)

¼ teaspoon salt

2 eggs, at room temperature

2½ teaspoons sugar

3 tablespoons melted butter

Filling

3 brandied peaches, sliced

3 brandied apricots, sliced

24 brandied red cherries

3 tablespoons Curaçao

3 tablespoons sugar

¾ cup brandy, warmed

6 heaping tablespoons vanilla ice cream

Place flour in a 2-quart bowl. Dissolve yeast in the warm water. Add yeast to the flour with the salt and one of the eggs. Beat *thoroughly* with an electric mixer at medium speed (about 2 minutes). Add the remaining egg and beat again about 2 minutes. Cover and set aside in a warm place (about 85°F.) to rise for 1 hour.

Beat together sugar and butter. Stir down batter and add butter mixture. Beat thoroughly. Cover and let rise 1 hour more. Grease six individual savarin molds (shallow, round molds with indented bottoms). Fill each mold one-third full with baba dough. Cover and let rise in a warm place until dough comes to the tops of the molds. Preheat oven to 450°F. Bake babas 15 to 20 minutes. To prepare filling, heat brandied fruits in a shallow skillet. Add Curaçao and sprinkle with sugar. Pour brandy over fruit and ignite. Place babas in individual serving dishes; spoon ice cream into cavities of babas and top with the hot fruit mixture. Serve immediately. Serves six.

This colorful flaming dessert may be prepared ahead of time. It cooks like a lovely volcano when it is served.

CASSATA ALLA SICILIANA VOLCANO
(SICILIAN VOLCANO CASSATA)

Ice Creams

½ cup vanilla ice cream

¾ cup chocolate ice cream

½ cup raspberry sherbet

Filling

½ cup heavy cream, whipped

1 egg white, stiffly beaten

¼ cup powdered sugar

½ cup finely diced, candied fruits

Topping

3 egg whites

1 tablespoon sugar

1 egg yolk

brandy

Put vanilla ice cream into a chilled 1½-quart mold. Use a spoon to smooth it evenly against the walls of the mold, leaving a slight hollow in center. Spread chocolate ice cream over the vanilla ice cream. Repeat with raspberry sherbet, making sure to leave a small hollow in center. (If ice cream becomes too soft to spread, place mold in the freezer to harden each layer before adding the next one.) Place mold in freezer while making filling: gently combine whipped cream and beaten egg white. Fold in sugar and fruits. Spoon into center of mold. Cover with foil and freeze for at least 6 hours. When ready to serve, prepare topping. Combine beaten egg whites with sugar and egg yolk. Reserve one-half egg shell. Preheat oven to 450°F. (very hot). Unmold ice cream onto a round platter and cover with topping mixture. A wet spatula works best to spread mixture. Place half-egg shell on top of ice cream mold and push it down into the ice cream until its edge is even with the top. Place platter in large baking dish on a layer of crushed ice. Place in preheated oven, and bake 3 to 5 minutes until topping is golden brown. When brown, remove from oven. Fill egg shell half with brandy; ignite and serve while still flaming. Serves six.

Choice stewed peaches are delicious prepared in a blazing syrup of Kirsch with vanilla ice cream.

PEACH FLAMBE

4 large peaches

3 cups water

½ teaspoon vanilla extract

6 tablespoons sugar

4 tablespoons Kirsch

*8 scoops vanilla ice cream
(2 scoops per serving)*

Peel skins from peaches and cut into slices. In a 2-quart saucepan, bring the water to a boil. Add vanilla and sugar, and stir well. Add sliced peaches and simmer until just soft. Remove peaches to a chafing dish. Pour 1 cup of the syrup in which the peaches have been cooked over the peaches. Light the burner of the chafing dish, and add 2 tablespoons Kirsch. Heat, basting slices constantly, until syrup is golden, about 15 minutes. Arrange ice cream on 4 individual plates. Spoon peaches over ice cream. Top each serving with 1½ teaspoons of the remaining Kirsch and ignite. Serve at once. Serves four.

CREPES FLAMBEES SARAH BERNHARDT

12 crêpes (see index)

1 cup cream cheese, at room temperature

2 tablespoons raspberry jelly

½ teaspoon grated lemon peel

½ teaspoon grated orange peel

juice of 1 lemon

2 tablespoons powdered sugar

3 tablespoons butter

2 tablespoons pineapple juice

2 cups washed and hulled strawberries

½ cup Curacao

2 tablespoons Kirsch

Prepare 12 crêpes (see index under Crêpes Suzette), and lay them flat on waxed paper. Mix cheese with raspberry jelly, lemon peel, orange peel, and lemon juice. Spread mixture evenly on crêpes and roll up. Arrange crêpes in a buttered ovenproof dish. Preheat oven to 300°F. Heat crêpes 5 minutes. Meanwhile, melt sugar in a crêpes suzette pan or small skillet, stirring constantly. When lightly browned, add butter; mix well, and add pineapple juice, strawberries, and Curaçao. Simmer for 30 seconds. Remove crêpes from oven; pour Kirsch over crêpes, and ignite. Ladle strawberries over crêpes and serve immediately. Serves four.

BANANE A LA OLD WHITE CLUB
(BANANAS OLD WHITE CLUB)

2 tablespoons powdered sugar

2 tablespoons butter

juice of 1 lemon

juice of 1 orange

2 tablespoons Grand Marnier

2 bananas, peeled and cut in half lengthwise

2 tablespoons rum

1 teaspoon cinnamon

vanilla ice cream, 2 scoops per serving

Melt sugar in skillet, stirring constantly. When lightly browned, add butter, lemon and orange juices, and Grand Marnier. Cook gently until mixture starts to bubble. Arrange banana halves in pan and roll them in the sauce several times to coat evenly. Reduce heat and simmer 3 minutes. Pour rum over bananas while still in pan and ignite. Sprinkle with cinnamon and serve with vanilla ice cream. Serves four.

LES FRAISES ROMANOFF
(STRAWBERRIES ROMANOFF)

2 quarts strawberries

1/3 cup sugar

½ cup Kirsch

½ cup Curaçao

1½ cups heavy cream, whipped and chilled

4 cups vanilla ice cream, softened

1 cup crumbled Macaroons (see index)

Wash and hull strawberries; put them in a bowl. Sprinkle with sugar and add Kirsch and Curaçao. Toss berry mixture. Chill for 1 hour. Fold softened ice cream into whipped cream, and then fold mixture into berries. Gently fold in crumbled macaroons. Serve immediately. Serves four.

Luscious black cherries conspire with flaming Kirsch to create a delightful after-dinner favorite.

CHERRIES JUBILEE

2 cups water

1 cup sugar

½ teaspoon vanilla extract

2 pounds cherries. washed, stemmed, and pitted

2 teaspoons cornstarch

½ cup Kirsch

4 teaspoons sugar

vanilla ice cream, 2 scoops per serving

Bring water to a boil in a 2-quart saucepan. Add 1 cup sugar, vanilla, and cherries; simmer 8 to 10 minutes. Dissolve cornstarch in 2 teaspoons cold water, and add to cherries. Cook and stir until slightly thickened. Remove from heat and add ¼ cup Kirsch. Place cooked cherries in a chafing dish over lighted burner. Sprinkle with 4 teaspoons sugar and the remaining ¼ cup Kirsch; ignite and serve flaming sauce over vanilla ice cream. Serves eight.

COFFEES

A good cup of coffee—however clichéd it may sound—is really the perfect end to an excellent meal. Sometimes people forget that there can be considerably more to coffee than just brewing and serving it. By adding spices and liqueurs, you can lift coffee from the drab, everyday experience it often is into a fitting climax to an outstanding meal.

Unless you have served a flambé or an unusually heavy dessert, an exciting coffee is in order. Even if you have prepared a complicated dessert, you might want to serve a coffee that is a little out of the ordinary. Among the recipes that follow, you will find both elegant coffees and slightly unusual ones. They are all favorites at The Greenbrier.

CAFE DIABLE

2 cinnamon sticks

10 cloves, heads removed

2 teaspoons whole coriander seeds

2 tablespoons coffee beans

16 lumps sugar

peel of 1 orange, cut into a spiral

peel of 1 lemon, cut into a spiral

¾ cup brandy

1 quart strong coffee

Light flame beneath café diable bowl or chafing dish to warm bowl. Add cinnamon sticks, cloves, coffee beans, and coriander. Rub sugar lumps over orange and lemon peels, and add to dish with the peels. Let all ingredients warm together for 3 or 4 minutes. Add half the brandy to the ingredients in the dish, and ignite. While the flame is still burning, reach into the dish with tongs; pick up peels, taking care not to burn yourself, and pour the remaining brandy down the peel spirals, letting the brandy flow off peels into bowl. Add coffee to brandy mixture and let flame a moment, dipping peels up and down until flames are extinguished. Ladle into hot diable cups or demitasse cups. Serves eight.

CAFE VIENNESE

4 cups strong hot coffee

sugar to taste

½ cup heavy cream, whipped

Pour coffee into four cups and add sugar. Mix well and top with a generous portion of whipped cream. Serves four.

IRISH COFFEE

8 teaspoons sugar

¾ cup Irish whiskey

4 cups strong hot coffee

4 tablespoons whipped cream

Heat 4 stemmed glasses by rinsing them with very hot water. Place 2 teaspoons sugar and 3 tablespoons whiskey in each glass. Slowly add *hot, strong* coffee, and stir to blend. Top each glass with 1 tablespoon whipped cream. Serves four.

Demitasse is the coffee served after dinner throughout France. Be sure to make at least double-strength coffee and to serve extra sugar with the demitasse.

DEMITASSE

6 demitasse-sized cups of strong, hot coffee

6 lumps sugar

peel of ½ lemon, cut in thin strips

Fill demitasse cups with strong coffee. Add one lump sugar to each cup and serve with thin strips of lemon rind. Serves six.

CAFE ROYALE

6 lumps sugar

6 cups strong, hot coffee

¾ cup Cognac

Drop a lump of sugar into each cup, and fill half way with hot strong coffee. Fill each cup with 3 tablespoons cognac. Ignite and serve flaming. Serves four.

BRAZILIAN MOCHA

5 tablespoons unsweetened cocoa

¼ teaspoon salt

5 tablespoons sugar

½ cup cold water

1 cup boiling water

1½ cups strong hot coffee

1½ cups half-and-half

¾ cup heavy cream, whipped

Combine cocoa, salt, sugar, and the cold water in a 2-quart saucepan. Stir until smooth. Bring to a boil, and simmer for 2 minutes. Gradually add the boiling water. Mix coffee with half-and-half and add to cocoa mixture. Bring to a boil, and beat with a rotary beater until frothy. Serve in heated cups topped with whipped cream. Serves six.

CAFE TURQUE
(TURKISH COFFEE)

8 tablespoons powdered coffee

8 tablespoons sugar

4 cups cold water

Place coffee in coffee pot (brass or copper pot works best). Add sugar and cold water. Heat and stir until mixture boils briskly; remove from heat and let boiling stop. Repeat boiling procedure three times. When finished, serve with a little cold water on the side. Serves four.

CAFE BRULOT CREOLE
(CREOLE COFFEE)

peel of 1 orange, cut into 6 pieces

peel of ½ lemon, cut into 3 pieces

2 cinnamon sticks, broken

15·whole cloves

15 lumps sugar

2/3 cup cognac

1 quart double strength coffee

Put orange and lemon peels, cinnamon, cloves, sugar, and ½ cup of the cognac in a chafing dish. Light burner and stir constantly until contents are warm. Ignite and slowly add coffee. Pour in remaining cognac. Ignite again and ladle blazing coffee into cups. Serves six.

CAFFE EXPRESSO
(EXPRESSO COFFEE)

12 tablespoons powdered Italian coffee
(preferably Madaglia D'Oro)

2 cups boiling water

peel of 1 lemon, cut in thin strips

Pour boiling water over coffee powder in top of coffee pot. Cover tightly so steam cannot escape. Let stand three minutes before serving. Serve lemon peels on the side. Serves six.

INDEX

275